Introductions in
Feminist Theology

5

Editorial Committee

Mary Grey
Lisa Isherwood
Catherine Norris
Janet Wootton

Sheffield Academic Press

Introducing a Practical
Feminist Theology of Worship

Janet H. Wootton

Copyright © 2000 Sheffield Academic Press

Published by Sheffield Academic Press Ltd
Mansion House
19 Kingfield Road
Sheffield S11 9AS
England

Printed on acid-free paper in Great Britain
by Cromwell Press Ltd,
Trowbridge, Wilshire

British Library Cataloguing in Publication Data

A catalogue record for this book is available
from the British Library

ISBN 1-84127-067-9

Table of Contents

Editors' Preface

BISFT is delighted to be working with Sheffield Academic Press in the development of an Introductions series. The forerunner, *Introducing Feminist Theology* (Sheffield: Sheffield Academic Press, 1993) was well received and provided a solid source at an academic level for those new to the subject. Its success provided the idea for a series of brief and relatively inexpensive books introducing aspects of feminist theology, presented by specialists but accessible to the average reader. *Introducing Redemption in Christian Feminism* by Rosemary Radford Ruether was the first, followed by Lisa Isherwood and Elizabeth Stuart's *Introducing Body Theology* (1998) and Melissa Raphael's *Introducing Thealogy: Discourse on the Goddess* (1999).

Janet Wootton's *Introducing Feminist Liturgy* covers the whole spectrum of women's participation in public worship, as leader, preacher, hymn-writer, scholar, as well as listener, singer and one who knows the connection between liturgy and life and the importance of making liturgy life-enhancing for women.

In keeping with the aims of the Introducing series, she provides a reliable guide to the history of thinking in the area of women and liturgy, examines current issues and outlines possible developments. Readers will undoubtedly be energized to re-think traditional ideas, and will find themselves empowered to bring about changes in their own practice.

Introduction

There are three great woman-songs in Scripture. Among all the plethora of Psalms, commonly ascribed to King David, or one of the sons of the Levites; among all the heroic accounts of battles passed down through the oral tradition of the Hebrew people; among all the soaring imagery of radical prophetic writing, three songs are ascribed to women.

How we would love to know what Miriam and her women companions sang when they danced in triumph on the shore of the Red Sea (Exod. 15.19-21). Instead, the truncated narrative of their ritual is dominated by the parallel account of Moses' song of victory (Exod. 15. 1-18). But we do know what Deborah sang after the victory over Sisera and, though Judges 5 ascribes the song to Deborah and Barak, her army commander, it is universally known as 'The Song of Deborah', the ascription to Barak being taken as a secondary addition to the text of Judges 5.

But even Deborah's song is overlaid by the patriarchal nature of its context. I recall a discussion during a meeting of the committee that compiled the hymnbook, *Hymns and Psalms* (Methodist Publishing House, 1983). The hymn under discussion was Christopher Idle's 'Powerful in Making us Wise to Salvation'—about Scripture. One line reads, 'Written by men borne along by the Spirit'. By this time, committee members' opinions were fairly well known and, when I drew breath to speak, everyone knew, or thought they knew, what my objection was going to be. 'Of course', someone said, 'unfortunately, it is probably true that it was all written by men—unless', and this scornfully, 'you think the song of Deborah was actually written by her'.

However, there is more wrong with the hymn line than its sexist language, and it goes to the heart of the issues raised by any feminist discussion of liturgy. I imagine that, in fact, Deborah's song is retained in the scriptural record because it was *written* by a man. The skill of writing as a means of preserving and passing on the narrative record of a people's history has nearly always been in the hands of men. It is characteristic of a hymnwriting tradition and the essentially literary task of compiling a hymnbook that 'written by men' is taken to be equivalent to 'originated by men'. The power of oral tradition is simply ignored. My objection to that line in Idle's hymn is not so much to the word 'men', as to the idea that the sole way of describing the formation of Scripture (implied, indeed, by the very word 'Scripture') is the process of writing.

In the case of Deborah's time of leadership, we have two accounts: the prose narrative of Judges 4 and the song of triumph in Judges 5. Of the two, the song is more likely to be in its original form, and reliable. John Gray writes, 'we must remember that a prose narrative is always more open to secondary additions and adjustments than a poetic version, which by its very nature demands to be incorporated as it stands' (Gray 1977: 164-65) Further, it is arguable that the song of Deborah is the oldest passage still existing in the Bible as we have it now.

As well as being a vivid and exciting account of the victory, the song of Deborah celebrates triumph almost entirely from the point of view of the women involved. Deborah appears as the answer to Israel's needs at a time of anarchy and decline, as 'a mother in Israel'. Kings and princes are called on to listen, but it is ordinary people, the traders whose way of life Deborah has restored and, in particular, the women drawing water, who commemorate the victory and pass the story from generation to generation (Judg. 5.11).

After a dramatic account of the battle, in which the disunity of the tribes is revealed, the final stroke of victory is in the hands of another woman. Jael's brutal act is told in loving detail; violence and sexual innuendo working together as Sisera's assumption of her hospitality literally rebounds on his own head. Verse 27 revels in the mighty king sinking down, his legs buckling, and lying prone at the feet of the tribeswoman. This is indeed a story which might be lasciviously passed around the gathering of the merry-makers at the places where they draw water.

In contrast with Jael's magnificent act of power, the humiliation of defeat is also portrayed through the eyes of women. There is breath-taking irony in the description of Sisera's mother and her ladies con-quering their anxiety by dwelling on the sweet fruits of victory. He must be, even now, dividing up the spoil—fine cloth to grace the victor's neck and, of course, all the women they could possibly want. There is unforgettable humour and poignancy in the delicate interplay between Jael's powerful action, and the anticipated downfall of the apparently powerful and wise women waiting for Sisera, caught even as they anticipate the humiliation of women such as Jael (vv. 28-30).

If this is truly a woman's song, for women and about women, some surprising principles begin to emerge. It is by no means gentle, or even squeamish about violence. It is ready to see overweening women humiliated, just as it celebrates the act of the woman in her tent.

Alternatively, there do seem to be some factors which mark out this song from other similar triumphal poems. For one thing, the song belongs with ordinary people in a way in which, for example, the song of Moses in Exodus 15 does not. The story begins with the disruption of ordinary life (Judg. 5.6) and calls upon the traders and drawers of water to carry the celebration of victory (vv. 10-11). The tribes of Israel are not glorified as a victorious united whole, as elsewhere in the stories of the judges, but their disunity is exposed as nowhere else. Even internal conflicts, such as the deep divisions within the tribe of Reuben, are not hidden (vv. 13-18). This is not an idealized account, like Gideon's sounding the trumpet to call an army of over 30,000 which had to be whittled down by God in case they claimed the victory for themselves (Judg. 7). In Deborah's song, the choice between the urgency of fighting and the necessity of day-to-day living is made quite clear.

There is also a delicacy of humour and skilful interweaving of irony which is not to be found elsewhere. This is in contrast with the simple narrative humour of the dialogue between Abram and Yahweh over the fate of Sodom and Gomorrah (Gen. 18.22-33) or Isaiah's heavy satire on the manufacture of idols (Isa. 44.12-20).

These are different kinds of markers and must be treated in different ways. Delicacy of touch and half-hidden humour are stylistic markers. To note these in this context is to suggest that there may be a female way of writing which arises from a female cast of mind or way of thinking. The argument has to be handled with care, since men as well as women are capable of delicacy of thought and ironic finesse. However, women's ways of communicating may be governed by social circumstances. If the only time you have to share stories in a public setting is when the women gather to draw water, your way of telling stories might be different from that of men, whose whole life would have been more public.

But concentration on ordinary life even in a triumphal song is a marker of content. While the great prophets of Israel proclaim God's will that the lowly should be treated justly and that oppressors be brought down, the triumph songs of women celebrate real examples of this principle. In a patriarchal society, when a woman wins a victory, this prophetic principle comes to reality. The woman becomes a sign that God's will has prevailed, a sign of hope for the future.

The second woman-song is Hannah's song of triumph (1 Sam. 2.1-10) after the birth and dedication of her son Samuel. It is written for the most part in the present tense. This is what happens when God's will is done. The old balance of pride and oppression is overturned as those who were despised are honoured and those who once boasted in their arrogance are brought low.

Towards the end, the future tense is used. The present reality becomes a promise for future generations. This is not something that will happen at some future unspecified date, but a process that has already begun. This is what it is like when God works.

Again, the language is not sentimental. Present reality and future hope both include judgment of the proud as well as honour for the weak. It is the overturning of the previous status quo, during which God's enemies triumphed while God's servants were despised. Now the barren Hannah gloats over her enemies, not because of what she has accomplished, but because God's will has prevailed. Human power or strength is not the criterion for success any more: 'Strong men stand in mute dismay' (v. 4). In the new situation it is God's judgment which is the deciding factor.

Of course, the most familiar of the triumph songs ascribed to women in Scripture is the song of Mary at the moment when she met her cousin Elizabeth, both women who were unexpectedly pregnant. This time it is not the previously barren Elizabeth who cries out her triumph, but Mary, whose pregnancy might have been a cause of great shame.

At the moment when Elizabeth tells Mary that the child leapt in her womb at Mary's voice, Mary sings her song of prophetic joy. Like Hannah, she sees her triumph as an example of God's purposes and a promise for the future. By looking with favour on his lowly handmaid, God shows what the might and holiness of God looks like in reality.

This time, the song is entirely in the past tense as Mary claims that God's promises have been fulfilled in entirety in the overturning of her low estate. By this action, God has routed the proud, brought down monarchs from their thrones, filled the hungry with good things and fulfilled the promise given to Abraham for his children's children. Surely all generations will call Mary blessed, if she has become the sign of God's radical alternative for all time.

What has happened, then, to this sparse but precious tradition of woman-songs in Scripture? There may, of course, be others. Much of the oral tradition that lies behind the early narratives may have been preserved and passed on by women. The proverbs and wisdom writings ascribed to Solomon may also have belonged to a female tradition at one time. Wisdom herself is a fascinating and unexpected figure. It is highly likely that women as well as men had a hand in passing on the Gospel narratives and it is entirely possible that the letter to the Hebrews might have come from the hand of Priscilla.

But staying for the moment with the songs ascribed to women and, in particular, with the most famous of them—the song of Mary—I would like to argue that the way in which subsequent generations have treated the song exemplifies a general response to the liturgical action of women, and of other marginalized groups.

By far the majority of the world's Christians over the full length of the Christian tradition have repeated Mary's song on a regular basis. *The Oxford Dictionary of the Christian Church* (Cross and Livingstone 1974) notes that it has been the canticle of vespers in the Western Church probably since St Benedict (c. 480–c. 550), and is sung daily in the morning office except on certain great feasts in the Greek Church. Certainly, for many generations, the words would have been encountered by most people in a language they did not understand. But a vast number of people have chanted, spoken or heard the song at least weekly.

The effect on the Christian churches as power bases in the world has been negligible! Far from bringing down the mighty from their thrones, the churches have joined them there. Christians, from ambitious bishops and popes to nineteenth-century industrialists, have sung these words on a Sunday and gone out to grind down the poor and starve their children during the following week.

The beauty and familiarity of the words in the Authorized Version of the Bible, used regularly in worship through the centuries, hides their radical power. They become sentimental, effete, everything that Mary's song is not. Aided by Christmas carols that sentimentalize Mary as the 'mother mild' and 'lowly maiden', Mary's song becomes a further weapon in the patriarchal arsenal which keeps women poor and lowly, rather than the cry of triumph which should overturn patriarchy and all other oppressive systems. The song is defused and made safe.

Throughout the history of the Christian tradition, there have, of course, been those whose devotion to Mary has shown itself in a humble and radical lifestyle. More recently, the Magnificat itself has given rise to a number of hymns which have rediscovered and celebrated its true message. In 1968, Fred Kaan wrote, 'Sing we the song of high revolt', entitled 'Magnificat now' to the tune TANNENBAUM, more commonly sung to the Red Flag. The last verse reads,

> He calls us to revolt and fight
> With him for what is just and right,
> To sing and live Magnificat
> In crowded street and council flat.[1]

The hymn and its tune caused something of a stir when it appeared in Galliard's *New Life* (Bailey 1971) for use in assemblies, clubs and churches. Kaan's text is far truer to the tenor of Mary's words than Timothy Dudley Smith's 'Tell out my soul the greatness of the Lord', written in 1961 and included in almost every major hymn collection since. Unfortunately, however, Fred Kaan's text removes the song from Mary and gives the initiative to Jesus who is described calling the present generation to respond to Mary's words. The link between the experience of the woman Mary and the song is broken.

At the fiftieth anniversary of Christian Aid in 1995, Michael Taylor, the Director of Christian Aid, decried the regular recitation of the Magnificat while the Christian churches were doing so little to witness to its words. He declared a 'Moratorium on Magnificat'. My text, 'When Mary heard her cousin say God's promises would be fulfilled', is an attempt to take the idea seriously. The middle two verses read:

> But while the poor support the proud
> And tyrants thrive in lands and homes
> And while the hungry people crowd
> Around the mighty on their thrones:
> While greed and need go on and on
> How dare we think of Mary's song?
>
> And when it comes to you and me
> To show the world a God who cares,
> We duck responsibility
> And hide ourselves behind our prayers.
> Till we have faced our common wrong
> How dare we think of Mary's song?[2]

---

1.   'Sing me a Song of High Revolt', Fred Kaan © 1968 Stainer & Bell Ltd, London, from *The Hymn Texts of Fred Kaan*.
2.   Published in *Magnet* 32 (1995): 14-15. © Janet Wootton.

As Mary is emerging into feminist and liberation theology as a figure of strength and courage, a symbol of God's reversal of oppressive roles, so her song has emerged over the last 30 years as a pattern for an alternative to the present patriarchal power structures.

What has happened to the woman-songs of the Bible is symptomatic of what happens to women's liturgical actions and words throughout the Christian tradition. In general they have been ignored. I have often sung about Samuel, but never about Hannah; David's song of triumph (2 Sam. 22) is a mine of imagery for hymns and prayers, but Deborah's song remains untouched. In general, the liturgical action of women is marginalized or ignored.

The exception in more recent centuries has been the work of women hymnwriters, though even these tend to be treated as a 'special case'. Sometimes their writing is rendered safe if it is not so already, especially where it refers to the taboo subjects of women's bodily functions. For example, the verse beginning with the quatrain,

> Enough for him, whom cherubim
> Worship night and day,
> A breastful of milk,
> And a mangerful of hay:

has been omitted from almost every major hymnbook in which Christina Rossetti's hymn, 'In the Bleak Midwinter' has been included.

This book seeks to rediscover the enormous wealth and vitality of women's liturgical writing and practice, as it appears in Scripture, as it continued, though often hidden and silenced, through the history of the Christian era, and as it is exploding into life in these days. Much of the content is derived from my own experience as a minister in one of the non-conformist Christian traditions. I have, of course, drawn on the writing and experience of many others in Christian or post-Christian traditions. There are many other stories to tell, encompassing the religious experience of women in many traditions.

Chapter One

Whispering the Liturgy

It is impossible to overestimate how effectively women have been silenced throughout human history, and the implications of this silencing in the loss to the human race of wisdom, creativity and development. Overwhelmingly, prominent figures in the fields of science, technology, the creative arts, politics, business entrepreneurialism and sport have been men. The conclusion commonly drawn has been that men occupy the extreme of genius almost exclusively. There are creative, entrepreneurial women, but they are almost never of that calibre which makes them front-runners in any field. Either that, or they do not have the drive or single-mindedness that turns genius into achievement. Women are suited to domestic life. It is men whose place is the public sphere, the active, risky, entrepreneurial life. In fact, they rely on the natural moderation of women to provide the domestic base from which to operate: 'Behind every successful man there is a woman'.

This extraordinary set of assertions complies with the incontrovertible fact of women's lack of outstanding public achievement. The fact that its extraordinary nature has not been perceived is a measure of women's lack of esteem. Generations of women have been brought up in a world in which all prominent figures of the present and the past, in the local and global sphere, were men. Further, they have been brought up either to believe that this is quite simply the proper state of affairs, or, when this moral argument was no longer tenable, to accept that all the evidence pointed to the natural mediocrity of women. At least, in this latter state of affairs, prominent women could be seen as statistical anomalies rather than being condemned as moral perversions. Whether patriarchy is a purely social construct, or the brutal distortion—amounting to a caricature—of genetic gender differences, the effect is to deprive women of the opportunity to develop their talents to the full, and to deprive the world of the benefit of those talents.

For the evidence could point, wholly or partially, to another conclusion. It could be that women almost never achieve prominence because they have been systematically denied any opportunity to do so, and have been vilified or idolized when they have done. Idolization, of course, has the same kind of negative effect as vilification, in that the successful woman is not seen as an example for others to follow and has the frustration of having her own real qualities overlooked.

If this second conclusion is even partially true, it is surely the most amazing act of brutality that the human race has ever inflicted on its own members. For human talent and creativity to be suppressed to this extent, the process must begin at birth. This is true for a large variety of people against whom there is discrimination. Throughout history, people have been stripped of their human dignity and denied the opportunity for education on the grounds of race, culture (indigenous peoples), class, disability and gender. This forms a complex matrix of discrimination, so that some people are subject to multiple suppression, while others are so embittered by their suffering in one area that they join in general hostility to another group. For example, the white working class male has been caricatured as a locus for racism, but 'Alf Garnett' is no more than an exaggeration, and is by no means a relic of the post-war years.

Ann O'Hara Graff, writing in *In the Embrace of God* (Graff 1995: 122-37), cites research by Carol Gilligan and others into girls' development. This research, based on two longitudinal studies with girls from 7 to 17, reveals a steady process of self-silencing. Graff writes:

> At the core of their findings is the phenomenon of girls giving up clear relationship with themselves and others based on what they know of feelings and interactions in favor of 'relationships' maintained by being nice and silencing what they know and feel. Their work documents the steady loss of connection to self and other through a process of self-silencing, shaped by our patriarchal culture, which gradually causes a diminution of authentic voice in order to accommodate oneself to the needs and feelings of others, especially men...A fine-tuned relational acuity, so clear in girls in middle childhood, erodes through adolescence until it is worn away into being the perfect young woman (1995: 125).

Given this specific and systematic suppression, it is not surprising that many women express their trauma in various forms of mental illness. Of course, this is generally seen as a further example of the weakness of women, and their unsuitedness to deal with the pressures of life in an independent way, rather than being regarded as their natural, human reaction to the crushing of their personality. My own experience of adolescence and young adulthood was of a barely containable anger against everything that seemed to conspire against the free adult life to which I aspired. If I expressed that anger, I was being a difficult teenager or a tiresome woman. I sought the role of an 'angry young woman' and found that there wasn't one. Even the rebellion of others of my generation was expressed in terms of the brotherhood of all mankind and had no real room for sisterhood of any kind.

The process of conscientization which leads to a rebellion against self-silencing begins with the recognition that it has taken place. Many women, particularly if they are otherwise privileged (that is, their suppression is only on the basis of gender), stoutly deny that they have ever known discrimination because they are women. The same women will feel comfortable with sexist language used in worship and elsewhere, and will be frankly puzzled by the anger of their sisters expressed against the effective hiddenness of women and women's experience in all walks of life.

But the process of conscientization is extremely painful, too. It involves, after all, a woman realizing the extent to which her own life has been crushed. Even worse, she recognizes the extent to which she has connived at the crushing of other women. There is blood on her hands, her own, and that of countless other women, denied the chance to live as fully human beings.

When she looks around to see what female humans might be like, in all their variety and achievement, she finds almost no female tradition in any field. To quote my own experience again, brought up in a household full of encouragement, and a church tradition in which women had been ordained for several generations, when I became aware of my own vocation to ministry I had never heard a woman preach, or known a church with a woman minister. It was only much later that I met Revd Elsie Chamberlain, a congregational minister ordained in 1941 who became my own 'heroine'. There was no tradition of women's preaching, liturgy or church leadership that I could recognize as a moulding influence on my own development.

June Boyce-Tillman quotes the same kind of experience in her own development as a musician. Interviewed for *Feminist Theology*, she said,

> if we had an unbroken tradition of women's music-making in Europe,
> instead of just isolated women, we might learn more about a woman's

style of writing... What we lack, and we lack desperately in our society, is that public corporate women's music-making tradition. There are isolated women, but women's public corporate music-making is systematically obliterated by the Church (1998: 113).

Silencing Women's Leadership

Women who wish to exercise scholarly or leadership roles of any kind in the Church face a double silence of tradition. As in other areas of life—the sciences, for example, or business—there is no tradition of leading or successful women. There is no way of knowing what ordinary women scientists or heads of industry would be like and, similarly, there is no way of knowing what ordinary women moderators or bishops would be like, since the few recent examples are, by definition, extraordinary.

In the Church, however, there is another silencing factor, which exists in a lesser form in other areas. There are powerful arguments to the effect that women are not meant to exercise these roles. In many churches, these arguments are overpowering; they overpower any women who might be called by God's or their own desire to exercise public or leading roles. It is not only that there *is* not, there *cannot be* any tradition of women's church music, liturgical leadership or leadership of a congregation. Schüssler Fiorenza claims to base the whole of her aim in feminist theology on her experience in the Roman Catholic Church. She comments that, 'Women are not only the "silent majority" but we are also the "silenced majority" in the Roman Catholic Church... This deliberate or unconscious silencing of women in the Church engenders our ecclesiastical and theological invisibility' (1985: 3). For her, the task of feminist theology is

> to interrupt the patriarchal silencing of women and to make women visible as God's agents of grace and liberation. It shows that the need to silence women and to make us invisible in male linguistic systems and theological frameworks will no longer exist when the Church transforms its patriarchal structures of superordination and subordination that are exclusive of women or can admit us only in marginal and subordinate positions (Schüssler Fiorenza 1985: 14).

In countries that have been exploited by European imperialism and manipulated by the missionary movements, the oppression of women is complex. The World Council of Churches' study programme which resulted in the publication of *In God's Image* (Crawford and Kinnamon

1983), gave rise to an unexpected reaction in an Indian Christian village. Several questionnaires had been distributed in preparation for the consultation, one of which caused a violent incident, 'the women arguing that Jesus spoke to them of liberation, the men claiming a scriptural warrant to beat the women and silence them in public' (Crawford and Kinnamon 1983: 90) The woman who had experienced this conflict argued that, 'Christianity may have made the traditionally low estate of women in Indian society even worse...because claims of male domination are now "supported" by sacred text' (Crawford and Kinnamon 1983: 90).

The quest of feminist theology as a theology of liberation is not new. From time to time, even within the Christian community over the last 2000 years, the vision of the transformed community has surfaced. One of the characteristics of Christianity from the time of Christ to the present day has been a dramatic tension between liberating women to speech and action, and oppressing them to silence and passivity. It is clear that women played an important part in the leadership of churches during the first century after Christ. It is equally clear that this was highly controversial. The letters that flew around the first churches show a chaotic situation in which women leaders were respected and honoured while, at the same time, the role of women was constantly narrowed and confined.

Women had been present in the community that gathered around Jesus. They played many central roles, not only as recipients and beneficiaries of the liberating teaching of the new community, but also as formative influences. The Syro-Phoenician woman's engagement in debate in defence of her daughter drew Jesus out into healing beyond the Jewish community. It was a woman who anointed the head of Jesus in front of the crowd at a dinner party, proclaiming his messianic presence. And, of course, it was women who stayed at his tomb and bore witness to his resurrection.

Women and men disciples were recipients of the Spirit of God at Pentecost and, in fact, the prophecy of Joel cited by Peter specifically includes daughters and womenservants as well as sons and menservants. In the new, Spirit-filled community, women and men provided leadership, accommodation and the prophetic voice in worship. Paul and his contemporaries struggled with women preaching, prophesying and praying in tongues or in the vernacular. In the end, it is the negative rulings that come out of the early churches' struggle that are remembered, not the exciting liberation and leadership which gave rise to them.

The trend continued. Elise Boulding comments, tellingly, that, in response to the teaching of Jesus, 'Something very remarkable nearly happened' (1992: 340)! The 'very remarkable' thing was that, 'For the first hundred years of the new era, women were everywhere leaving behind old constraints, stepping into the public sphere, and participating in the creation of a new society' (1992: 10). But the 'nearly' grew more and more distant as a growing hierarchy and power structure in the church enforced silence in every way that it knew.

As the institutional church developed more and more exclusive rites, small dissenting communities kept alive the egalitarian tradition that emanates from the life and teaching of Jesus. Many of these communities honoured femaleness in their view both of humanity and of divinity, a trait which rendered them anathema to the patriarchal, deeply defensive institutional church. The new movements were universally condemned.

Development of women's authority and development of a radical theology went hand in hand. The Gnostic gospels list four female apostles in the list of twelve, perhaps reflecting a section of the Christian community which permitted equal partnership to men and women. Many of the mediaeval groups of women claimed authority to teach and interpret the scriptures. Perhaps the most startling were the thirteenth century Guglielmites, who proclaimed salvation through a female saviour. Guglielma of Milan was taken to be a female incarnation of the Holy Spirit, whose role was to bring in a new community with entirely female leadership, through which salvation would come to the whole world.

Groups of religious sisters were formed, devoted to the monastic life, and to a large extent autonomous in their leadership of worship. Prominent among these, of course, is the convent of Hildegard of Bingen, who wrote prolifically for her own community, developing a distinctive musical and theological style. Hildegard combined a powerful political influence with her religious life and it is poignant that, when she was in dispute with the Church over the burial of an excommunicated man, the sanction was the silencing of her house. Her ability to make music was, for a while, taken away.

Women also chose independent religious life as an alternative to the expected roles of marriage and childbearing which were so often part of a family's operation within the network of power in a community. Women might live in religious communities, bound by simple rules, or as anchoresses alone or attached to communities. During the European Middle Ages, there was a tremendous development of women's religious fervour. Movements such as the Beguines on the European continent and the anchoress movement in England provided opportunities for women to live lives devoted to service of God in the community, or to a secluded visionary existence.

These were not centrally organized, and were devoted largely to social care. Fiona Bowie describes their appearance as 'a genuinely new phenomenon in the life of the church...a loose movement, an impulse springing up spontaneously in many different areas' (1995: 16). Their desire was, 'to live a life of prayer, service and simplicity, free of male control either in the form of a priest or a husband' (Bowie 1995: 16). As well as their lifestyle, their worship was radical, consisting of intense devotion to Jesus, sometimes resulting in receiving the stigmata. All of these elements led to their exclusion from the Church by the Council of Vienne in 1311.

At the same time, women retained their position as repositories of wisdom within secular communities. 'Wise women' were healers and midwives, combining a knowledge of the use of herbal medicine with a deep sense of natural and supernatural power. Wisdom and ritual were passed from mother to daughter or from wise woman to protégée through the generations. Often the wise woman was feared for her power by the very community that relied upon her knowledge, and she may have lived alone on the edge of the community, an isolated and suspect individual.

Many local and domestic rituals would have included the participation of women: for example, rituals surrounding birth and death; celebrations to mark the passing of the seasons; and rituals to ensure success of agrarian and domestic life. Many of these took on a superficially Christian veneer. For example, the veneration of saints and martyrs often started as a way of honouring the holy lives of people within the community. Very often stories of holy lives built on pre-Christian traditions connected with natural features, such as springs or woods. Gradually, the shrines of men and women saints became more widely known and, by this means, community devotion developed at specific sites. These included oral narrative of the legend connected with the site, and songs in praise of the named saint.

But women's voices could not be allowed to be heard. Women could not be left in control of Christian or secular/pagan rituals. The women religious were forced into successively more repressive cloistering. The papal constitution 'Periculosa' of Pope Boniface VIII (1298), and the constitution 'Circa Pastoralis' of Pope Pius V (1566, following the Council of Trent) imposed a profession of vows entailing enclosure on all women religious. Communities of women religious who preferred simple vows were not allowed to receive novices and died out.

The secular or pagan wise women were dealt with more harshly. As a way of stamping out the old religions, women were branded as witches and hanged or burned. Drawing strength from the widespread suspicion and fear of powerful women in peasant communities, a wave of witch trials swept across Europe. Men as well as women were denounced, tried, often with torture, and executed. But the wave was directed against women and the knowledge of women. Thousands were burnt and destroyed, their voices silenced and their power lost for generations to come.

Their treatment is horrifying in that it demonstrates the misogyny that exists at every level of society. The malicious neighbour denounced the ugly old woman, who seemed so strange, to the parish priest, who was afraid of her power. He reported her for torture and condemnation by a Church and State in which women were seen as existentially evil, a fact that was enshrined in a whole web of misquoted Scripture and misap-propriated neo-Platonism and Aristotelianism. What chance did she stand? Raphael comments that 'the ferocious energy with which the patriarchal sacred has set upon the female sacred by naming it as profane and therefore marginalizing it, screening it off, secluding it, or (during the Witchcraze) torturing it into invisibility, is also an admission of its power' (1996: 49). She goes on, 'Perhaps spiritual feminism wants to say that women's exclusion from the cult has been less because they are too profane, but partly because patriarchy has sensed that they are *too sacred* and so would disorder the false sanctity of their own cult' (Raphael 1996: 49; her italics).

Silencing Women's Voices

But it is not just women's leadership, autonomy or authority that has been denied. The actual voices of women have been silenced, systemati-cally and effectively, through the large part of the history of the Christian Church.

In the Roman Catholic and Anglican traditions, the way this has happened is perhaps exemplified most clearly in church music. What has happened to women's singing is a specific instance of a general move away from informal, domestic, participatory worship and church life, towards a system which is formal (in the sense of following set forms), institutional and dominated by an exclusive leadership. The pattern is familiar and is repeated throughout the history of Judaeo-Christian worship, from the centralization of the cult on the Temple in Jersualem recorded in the Hebrew Scriptures to the institutionalization of the 1970s house churches in the 1990s ecumenical movement. There has been a desire to control and organize spiritual life, so that the dangers inherent in allowing freedom to the human or divine spirit can be mitigated or, at best, eliminated by institutional management.

There is very little evidence of forms of music in worship in the very early years of the Christian Church. The Jewish synagogue tradition allowed only male voices to be heard in the conduct of the liturgy, and the Temple tradition was based on a male hereditary priesthood, which included control of all sacred music. There is some evidence of women as well as men singing in Jewish charismatic sects. Philo of Alexandria describes the Therapeutae in Egypt, an ascetic sect, part of whose Pentecostal ritual involved bands of men and women dancing and singing throughout the night.

Some Christian groups, in the context of developing theology and worship, also included male and female singing and dancing. Gradually, these groups came to be condemned as heretical. Many came under the label of Gnosticism, though opposition to them was not only on theological grounds. As the official line began to be drawn, it became clear that freedom of expression in worship, and, above all, the participation of women, was in itself a bar to acceptance. Allowing women to exercise leadership was seen as integral to a whole network of dangerous freedoms which should be subdued by the force of institutional authority.

By the fourth century, choirs existed to lead worship, consisting of clerks in minor orders and boys. As education became the prerogative of the Church, church and cathedral choirs became the sole providers of musical education and sole arbiters of musical orthodoxy. There were still some places where women could participate in ritual music, but these were gradually brought under the Church's governance.

Local and domestic rituals, which were often in the hands of women would have included singing—lullabies, for example, and keening and wailing when laying out the dead. Gradually, both local and domestic rituals were incorporated into the institutional life of the Church. Daily prayer was taken into monastic life or incorporated into the work of the parish priest, with the women now as a silent audience. The sanctity of birth was replaced by the need to purify women after birth, which denied the wholesomeness of the natural process and effectively silenced the women, making them passive recipients of the Church's ministry rather than active participants in liturgical action.

Almost throughout the whole history of the institutional Church, music and worship has been in the hands of religious professionals, who have been men or boys. As church music grew in complexity, during the sixteenth century, occasionally women were permitted to sing in choirs. As women could not be permitted to enter the choir stalls because of their proximity to the altar, choirs with women singers were moved to the back of the church, to the gallery, where their voices could be heard but their bodily presence was as far removed as possible from the sanctuary.

The Second Vatican Council had a revolutionary effect on Roman Catholic liturgy. The Latin Mass was banned in favour of worship in the vernacular language of the community. The priest no longer faced away from the congregation to celebrate the Mass, but turned to face them. A focused attempt was made to engage the congregation far more in participatory worship, and this has had an effect on the architecture as well as the liturgical style of Roman Catholic churches in the last 20 years.

With the revival of the folk tradition, and a deliberate attempt to encourage congregational participation in worship, the voices of women are now being heard to a greater extent. It is, perhaps, only symbolically significant that Vatican II was the first Council of the Roman Catholic Church that women were permitted to attend. After vigorous lobbying for women to be present, 15 Catholic women from different parts of the world were invited. Such a small number, their contribution limited to sessions at which questions regarding women were being debated, could hardly have had a profound effect on the decisions which so radically changed Roman Catholic worship. Indeed, it is symptomatic that the new openness and participatory style still sub-consciously left women out of account.

The practice of Roman Catholic parishes has sometimes been more liberal than the strict letter of Vatican II. Beth Theobald comments that, 'training for specific ministries within the liturgy was sidelined by the

Bishops because the training envisaged led to minor orders from which women are barred … Rather than bar women from the ministries the method of training and status were dropped' (1997). In many churches now, music groups, worship groups and choirs consist of women and men, though formal church choirs of men and boys still exist.

However, in the English context, the male choir is most at home in the churches and cathedrals of the Anglican tradition. A great step has been taken in recent years in the admission of girls alongside boys. But women as mature singers are still largely silent. June Boyce-Tillman laments the lack of respect given to the mature woman's voice. She says, 'The grown woman's voice is still not there. It has to be the pre-pubescent girl's voice. As soon as it becomes a woman's voice, it is rejected' (1998: 114). And she tells the story of a colleague of hers, 'who was admitted to an order and had been a Lieder singer. She thought that the greatest gift she had to offer to God was her singing voice. But when she sang in the style that she'd sung for Schumann, in the Convent, she was told that this was inappropriate. Women's communities tend to sing in that pre-pubescent girl's type sound' (Boyce-Tillman 1998: 114).

The only place where the mature woman's voice has been honoured and respected has been in the Free Church traditions. There, choirs have traditionally been mixed, and have consisted mainly of adult singers, male and female. Their task has been to provide leadership in the singing of hymns and to sing anthems or other set pieces during worship. Children's choirs or singing groups have often been separate from the adult singers and have sung at their own point in the service. The tradition of the 'Sacred Solo', very much part of the evangelistic Free Church traditions, still exists. This used to be part of every sisterhood or women's guild meeting and, though it is delining with the decline of such meetings, songs are still being written for the mature woman soloist within these traditions. There is a genuine and live tradition of mature women's singing here, which is frequently ignored as Free Church traditions tend to be within our Anglican-dominated culture.

Within the black worship traditions, there is a strong and current tradition of women singing, either in mixed choirs or alone. The tradition of gospel singing has its origins in the music of defiance and solidarity amid the horrors of slavery and in indigenous musical traditions in Africa. Under the experience of slavery, women and men developed rituals such as the 'ring shout' and prayer meetings which, Diana L. Hayes writes, were very different from, 'the cold, stilted and artificial atmosphere of the enforced prayer meetings held by the slave master on their plantations which slaves were required to attend and to "behave" at while learning lessons on their inferiority yet "suitability" for slavery forced upon them' (1995: 23). In the present day, a Baptist minister, Joy Bostic, is working on a womanist theological methodology based on jazz music and its culture (Williams 1995: 124).

But if many of the Western traditions have silenced women's voices by controlling them, the Eastern tradition still silences them by exclusion. The liturgy of the Eastern Church became fixed at a far earlier date than that of the West. The worshipping church was, and is, seen as participation in the eternal worship of heaven. Liturgy echoes the words of the Trisagion and adds human praise of holy wisdom, the blessed Trinity, the mother of God and the saints. There are female figures in the liturgy—wisdom, Mary, Jerusalem, many of the saints—and these are represented in iconography as well as in words. But the voices that are heard are male.

Describing what is her own tradition, Leonie B. Liveris describes a poignant scene:

> In many churches, women and men sit separately, often the women up-stairs away from the men. The cantors are men, except on high days when women may sing in the choir, as are the readers, who chant the psalms and prayers and read the epistle, those who process the icons and carry the candles. Their sons are altar boys...Women are passive in the pews, for the responses to the prayers are left to the chanters, but their voices can often be heard whispering the liturgy, which they know so well from decades of faithful attendance (1995: 160-61).

I find this an intensely moving picture, and symbolic of women's silence in every part of life. In a parody of Plato's *Republic*, I visualize another cave. This cave is very beautiful and comfortable with the comfort of ages. People are not in chains, but are active all along the front wall of the cave. They are busy painting beautiful scenes, writing wonderful words. Here and there are groups of people engaged in lively debate. Their eyes are shining and their animated hand movements show that they are fully engaged in the debate. Elsewhere, heads are bent over serious experiments to help cave-dwellers to improve their lives. They have made huge advances in recent years and they are sleek with success.

In front of all this activity is a line of interpreters. They are staring into the dark depths of the cave, and explaining the activity behind them. In simplified and entertaining terms, the interpreters do their work. The same phrases come out again and again: 'It's good for you'; 'Look how beautiful it is'; 'aren't these people wonderful?'.

But who are they addressing? Now we see who is in chains. Facing the interpreters and occasionally catching a glimpse of the active people is a line of chained women. Now we realize that the active people and the interpreters are all men. The women vary enormously in appearance. Some are richly dressed; others are in rags. Some look at each other; others stare, longing to get past the interpreters to see the action. From them comes a sound like the rustle of dry leaves, or the rush of burning. The women are whispering the words of the interpreters: words they know so well, the only words they are allowed to speak.

What happens if the chains start to break, or the women start to raise their voices? If, instead of whispering the liturgy of others, women start to speak their own words? What happens is that the institution fights back!

Breaking the Silence

Attempts to release the voices or the creativity of women in liturgy are routinely met with hostility. This is true in Orthodox, Catholic and Protestant churches. Hostility comes from a wide variety of theological positions and starts from the very mildest forms of inclusive worship. For generations, women and girls have been hidden by the language of liturgy. Most references to human beings are to 'men' or 'brothers'.

The grammatical argument is that, in the English language, a company of people including male and female can be referred to using only a masculine noun or adjective. This is a language rule borrowed, like so much English grammar, from Latin. In Latin, nouns and adjectives fall into declensions which have grammatical gender, that is, all nouns are either masculine, feminine or neuter, and adjectives become masculine, feminine or neuter to agree with the nouns they are describing. Therefore it is impossible to use a noun or adjective without some reference to grammatical gender. In such a language, it is true that a collection of males and females are generally described by a noun or adjective with a masculine ending. This Latin rule is applied to English, where different words are the normal way of distinguishing gender, many words being non-gender-specific.

Words such as 'believers', 'sinners' and 'friends' are not gender-specific, though they would be in Latin and other similar languages. However, 'men', 'brothers' and 'mankind' refer specifically to male human beings. Women who were accepted for the ministry in the earliest days of women's ordination, the 1920s to 1940s, found that they were denied funding for their training on the grounds that the relevant trusts referred to 'men' and not 'men and women'. The word 'men' was taken strictly to apply to male humans only. In my own time, all official references to ministers were to men. I was able to interpret that as inclusive of women ministers until I attended a Spring School for ministers 'and their wives'—of course, 'men' have 'wives'. The language not only hid women, it hid the innate sexism of the language itself. It was simply not true that when most people said 'men' they meant 'men and women' in equal measure.

For all of my childhood and early adult years, I sang hymns and said prayers that made no reference to my own identity. The only reference to my gender was in the introduction to the children's address, which was to 'boys and girls' and the occasional hymn which used the non-gender-specific word 'children'. Once again, pre-pubescent females were all right, but mature women were hidden, excluded by the language.

Despite this, discussion of inclusive language in most traditional church circles is met with blank incomprehension or irritation with the issue. The label, 'political correctness', defines attempts to encourage inclusive language as manipulative language control and immediately vilifies the attempt and closes the discussion. The following incidents, drawn from my own experience over 20 years as a practitioner of liturgical and ecclesiastical development will, I am sure, chime with the experience of many readers.

Hymns and Psalms (1983) was the first denominational hymnbook to be published in England for a generation and therefore one of the first to face the issue of inclusive language. A group of women was invited to make a presentation to the editorial committee on the subject, and the committee treated the matter with proper seriousness. However, few changes were made. Only inclusive language referring to human beings was considered. And when the subject was raised at subsequent meetings, it was greeted with laughter.

If inclusive language about human beings gives rise to irritation or mockery, inclusive language about God is often met by an amazingly hostile response. In March 1996, for my induction service as President of the National Free Church Women's Council, I chose Judith Driver's hymn, 'Dance, dance, dance'. The hymn focuses on the Spirit of God, with the lively chorus, 'Dance, dance, dance, let the Spirit move you,/ Dance, dance, dance, moving from within,/ Dance, dance, dance, open up your heart to/ All the treasure that's within'. The verses describe the Spirit's effect on the worshipper, very much in terms of the prophetic call to justice in Isa. 61.1-3, quoted by Jesus to devastating effect in Lk. 4.18-19. True to the gender of *ruach* in the Hebrew Scriptures, in the last verse, the feminine pronoun is used—the only time the hymn uses a pronoun for the Spirit: 'Celebrate all the Spirit does,/ Celebrate all she does with us,/ Dance and sing, join us on the way,/ Dance and sing with us today'.

Everybody enjoyed the hymn, joining in movements I had devised for the chorus with great enthusiasm. The dancing theme was what appeared in reports of the service and seemed to have set a mood of celebration and hope.

Later, the General Secretary of the Free Church Federal Council, Revd Geoffrey Roper, intimated to me that he had received a letter from the General Secretary of the Assemblies of God, deploring the use of the feminine gender for the Holy Spirit as unscriptural and something he and his fellows could not condone. He hoped—and this is the irony—that the matter had escaped the notice of the people organizing the service, because the Moderator had, at the time, been ill. In other words, he suggested that the President of the Women's Council's naive theology had slipped through the wise net of Free Church 'orthodoxy'. Revd Kathleen Richardson, who was at that time the first woman moderator of the Free Church Federal Council, was amused. But, despite the satisfaction of being able to write back about the feminine gender of the Spirit in the Hebrew of the first testament, my enjoyment at the celebratory start to my presidency was marred.

Finally, 1988–98 was declared by the World Council of Churches to be the 'Decade of the Churches in Solidarity with Women'. This was met, largely, with indifference, contempt or tokenism on the part of the churches. In *Who Will Roll the Stone Away?*, Mercy Oduyoye records the years leading up to the declaration of the decade, when the women's desk of the WCC moved its emphasis from women's involvement in the churches to global issues of women's rights. She recalls the response: 'Sexism? What has it to do with ecumenism? There were lots of sniggers, and the churches relaxed yet further. None of this was seen as

threatening, for the issues were perceived as being non-theological'
(1990: 3).

I encountered the same sniggering reaction when the decade was
drawing to a close and Jean Mayland, the Associate Secretary for the
Community of Women and Men in the Council of Churches for Britain
and Ireland (CCBI now CTBI, Churches together in England and
Ireland), made a presentation to the Church Representatives Meeting.
This is a regular meeting of some 50 or more people drawn from the 32
member churches, 5 of CCBI, with the intention that they are 'the
people who can get things done'. They tend to be general secretaries of
the free churches and bishops in the hierarchical churches.

The presentation was followed by small-group work and then a plenary session. Questions for discussion included theological questions,
such as the inclusiveness of the 'image of God', practical matters con-
cerning women and violence, and matters of church practice. The small
group in which I was involved professed not to understand the theological question. This was not because they were theologically illiterate, or,
indeed, would have professed ignorance about any other theological
question. In the matter of church practice, several came from denominations that ordained women, and therefore could not see that there was
an issue. One pastor of a black majority church claimed that women had
completely equal status and could do everything except going up to the
altar, which actually excluded them from sacramental leadership.
However, he said, the women themselves are very happy with this,
since the 'fathers' had ordained it.

This aggressive 'so what's your problem' attitude was carried back
into the plenary session, where the sniggers began. A room full of adult
men and some women began to break apart as if the men were adoles-
cents and the women hags. In the end, a man stood up and said, quietly,
that he thought the argument should be carried on with more dignity as
befitted the subject. All honour to him, but the damage was done. The
women, whose voice is sparsely enough represented in the Church
Representatives Meeting, were silenced. The subject will be raised again
only with difficulty. Indeed, attitudes since the end of the decade have
made it quite clear that the subject has now been 'dealt with' and the
churches need think about it no longer. If a discussion about racism had
been conducted in the same manner, or if the subject of racism were
dismissed as lightly, there would be a justifiable outcry.

A great deal of the thrust of women's liturgy has been to do with breaking the silence. It is a theme that pervades this book, from redis-covering and constantly re-rediscovering the female presence in Scripture, through unearthing and retelling the stories of women's roles in the development of Christianity throughout these long repressive 2000 years, to patiently opening ears, hearts and communities, to the experiences and stories of women today.

The result is an explosion of grief and anger, celebration and joy. Women's stories are revolutionary in themselves. That is why they have been so long silenced. They are revolutionary because they come, for the most part, from the underside of history, from the margins, from the very places where the revolutionary ministry of Jesus was to be found. Our hymns, our rituals and our writings are alive with the zeal and excitement of the new community.

Chapter Two

Inter-action

The explosion of grief and anger, celebration and joy, which has broken the centuries' long silence of women, has resulted in a huge outflow of new worship material and new thinking about worship. The wealth and variety of liturgical expression and its impact on forms of leadership, styles of worship and even design of church buildings over the last decades cannot be overstated.

Feminist Christian worship forms a continuum within which a whole variety of elements interact. The life-experience of the participants interacts with the traditions; the individual, the community of participants and the wider community are all in tension during an act of worship; the words, symbols and even the space in which worship takes place work together to form the experience of worship.

These points of interaction may result in destructive rather than creative tension. A worship space that forces the participants to sit in rows, leaving any worship leaders with no choice but to be at the front, facing the others, may abnegate any non-patriarchal intention in worship. Failure, in an otherwise well-crafted and feminist act of worship, to refer to a major disaster that is on everybody's mind may disconnect worship from the life-experience of the participants. Or an ill-chosen ancient or modern text may destroy in a moment an atmosphere of worshipping in community.

This last example often happens when a Bible translation is used in worship which is different from the one used in preparation, and which mistranslates a word or translates it exclusively. For example, the word *adelphoi* is often wrongly translated as 'brothers', when its context clearly indicates that there were 'sisters' in the reference too. Alternatively, a modern liturgical text may be chosen, on the strength of its first line or general thrust, without noticing that it slips in a reference to 'men' as it proceeds. Many excellent, thought-provoking modern hymns were originally written from the point of view of the 'brotherhood of man'. In general, these will have been re-written in inclusive language, often by their original author once his or her consciousness of inclusive language was raised.

A good example of this is Brian Wren's hymn, 'Lord Jesus if I Love and Serve my Neighbour'. This excellent and radical text was originally written with entirely male references. But Wren re-wrote the second verse, with startling impact. It now reads, 'When I have met my sister's need with kindness,/ and prayed that she might waken from despair,/ open my heart, if, crying now for justice,/ she struggles for the changes that I fear'. The radical nature of the words is given an entirely new focus with the change from 'brother', which in this context was intended to be general, to 'sister'.

To maintain connectivity between individual and community, symbol and space, words and meanings, people of many different disciplines need to be engaged in shaping worship. This happens during the act of worship, if the full experience of the participants is engaged. But people of many disciplines also need to collaborate in providing material for worship, shaping spaces for worship, ensuring that feminist theology is accessible in worship, bringing the call for justice and the cry of the oppressed into worshipping life through material which grasps current political or ethical issues.

Very often, the very dynamism of feminist worship generates new material drawing on the talents and expertise of people who would not have thought themselves the 'type' to contribute to the development of worship. From Latin America comes the call that, 'The creativity demonstrated in liturgy, methods, content and modes of presentation is noteworthy. That is why we believe that women theologians, pastors, liturgical specialists and teachers of theology must work together' (Tamez 1995: 89). To the list I would add women architects, designers, politicians, medical practitioners, historians, educators...

Scholarship for Worship

There is, currently, a vast explosion of new material for worship being written. New liturgies, new hymns, new dramas for worship, new symbols and images, new use of worship space—all make up an experience of worship which has a chance of healing, challenging and changing the world.

Liturgical material is accompanying feminist theology in rediscovering or reinterpreting our heritage. New hymns are written about women in Scripture; from Scripture also come previously hidden female images of God as images or symbols for worship; the annals of history provide women whose lives we can celebrate in word and song; and women's experience as well as men's shapes our worship and challenges injustice.

This process can be seen in relation to two symbolic female characters in Scripture, Eve and Mary. Eve and Mary have been traditionally used to tell the symbolic story of women's fall and salvation, while Adam and Jesus have been used to tell 'men's' story. Of course, 'men's' story has been taken to be at the same time normative for all humans and exclusive of women, who need their own story. The figure of Eve has been used to typify women's terrible weakness and responsibility for all human misery and sin. Eve sinned first; the serpent went to Eve as representative of human fallibility based on emotion and desire, the more likely of the two first humans to be tempted.

Mary, on the other hand, has been used to demonstrate the value of feminine virtues. She has been represented as the ideal of meek obedience and patient suffering. For Protestants, she is a model of feminine obedience—the one who said 'Yes' to God. But in the Roman Catholic Church, she has become a cultic figure, co-redemptrix with Christ, herself immaculately conceived and the theological symbol in which women find their imago, where men find it in God. Schüssler Fiorenza writes, 'The cult of Mary in the Catholic church provides us with a tradition of theological language which speaks of the divine reality in female terms and symbols. This tradition encompasses the myth and symbols of the Goddess religion and demonstrates that female language and symbols have a transparency towards God' (1992: 139).

Thus the figure of Mary becomes a reason for not seeking the imago Dei of women in God. I had not understood this until I spoke at a diocesan study group in Kemsing, deep in the Kent commuter belt. I naively spoke of female imagery of God, supported by Scripture and tradition. Used to the ire of evangelical Christians, borne of straightforward misogyny, I was unequipped to meet the hostility of Anglo-Catholics, for whom the sole place for women to look was to Mary and, in particular, to the 'Stabat Mater', Mary beside the Cross of Jesus. Why, they wanted to know, was there not sufficient for me in this? Evangelical Christians wish us to find our imago in a male God, and Catholic Christians in a female human!

But the stories of both Eve and Mary can be retold by women. It is important that this is done at every level. Eve's story has been re-translated as part of a new translation of Genesis by Mary Phil Korsak. This very accurate translation makes clear the relationship between the different words used for human beings, which are confused in most English versions, in which 'man' is used to translate both *'adam'* and *'ish'*. In Korsak's version, 'Adam' is translated as 'groundling', so that Gen. 1.27 reads, 'Elohim created the groundling in his image, created it in the image of Elohim, male and female created them'.

The groundling is neither male nor female in gender. Korsak uses the neuter pronoun, 'it', all the way from Gen. 1.26 to 2.23, where the groundling is put to sleep and the 'counterpart' is taken from its side. Now, in Hebrew, for the first time, the words for man and woman, *'ish'* and *'isshah'*, are used. Male and female, in both creation accounts, are created simultaneously. There is no male until there is female and, significantly, there is no pre-existent male form from which the female is taken, though Genesis 2 does give the male priority in that moment of their creation.

In C. Christ's and J. Plaskow's *Womanspirit Rising*, Phyllis Trible looks again at Eve's story. She rehearses the biblical scholarship, but then moves on to re-tell the story from a woman's point of view. She asks, 'Why does the serpent speak to the woman and not to the man? Let a woman speculate' (Trible 1992a: 79). In the two encounters—the woman's with the snake and the man's with the woman—it is the woman who appears more thoughtful and active. She argues with the snake and is convinced. The snake knows that she will need to be convinced by rational argument and tries no other means. In the end, reason and desire come together and the woman reaches out and takes the fruit. She acts on her own volition. The serpent does not give her the fruit. She is active throughout.

On the other hand, the man makes no argument. He is given no reason for taking the fruit. He is given the fruit by the woman. He is passive throughout his part in the story. Trible comments, 'If the woman be intelligent, sensitive and ingenious, the man is passive, brutish and inept. These character portrayals are truly extraordinary in a culture dominated by men' (Trible 1992a: 79).

The complex of symbolism which forms the setting for Eve's story has been creative in providing material for worship. She is connected with the earth, the garden. She takes the decision that alters the course of creation. She bears the curse in the pain of childbearing. In a powerful one-woman show, drawing imagery from the Hebrew Scriptures among a great many other sources, Peri Aston, story-teller, re-plays the contentment of Eve's existence in the garden before it is spoiled by the rapaciousness of the male. For her, the woman and the garden are one.

In the Netherlands in the 1980s, the newly formed Women in Church and Society section of the Reformed Church published the magazine *Woman and Word*. The recognition of how male-centred hymnody was gave rise to a regular column known as 'Eva's Lied' ('Eve's Song'), under the editorship of Marijke Koijck-de Bruijne, encouraging the writing of feminist hymns and songs.

Eventually, so much material was gathered that a series of books was published under the same title. The compilers see the books as the record of a journey, 'towards a world where all people, women and men, are completely equal, because both women and men are created in God's image... The discovery, that as a female human being you have your rightful place, can be so liberating that you want to sing about it.' (Hilten 1984: 11) All that Eve has been seen as denying—the equal creation of women and men in God's image, the full humanity of women—is restored as Eve begins to sing her own song.

A song to Eve is the first in the collection and I quote it in full, in a translation by Frances Brienen of the Council for World Mission.

> Eve, your name means 'life',
> gift from God given to us
> who have been created in God's image.
> Related to you are all women
> and men who are building a world
> where life can be lived for real (genuinely).
>
> To tend God's earth like a garden,
> to protect her from exploitation and exhaustion
> and to work for a society
> in which inequality of sexes
> in word and deed and thought
> have disappeared, are we God's image.
>
> Ominously the future grins at us,
> tenaciously we choose the roads
> where Wisdom and God's Spirit pass.
> Where dreams that have become reality
> enter evil and light it up,
> there, Eve, we experience your name (Hilten 1984: 13. permission sought).

There is room for much creative encounter here. What was the nature of Eve's choice, and the significance of her conversation with the enigmatic serpent? What was her experience of coming to creation? Her name means 'life': what significance does that have for women today who face the horrors of racism, war and famine and manage to hold life together nonetheless? Can Eve stand up proud and strong, or is she solely the archetypal sinner?

The apple also features from time to time in liturgy and song, immediately recalling Eden, even though Genesis does not mention the type of fruit. Sydney Carter's amazing song, 'It Was on a Friday Morning', questions the fairness of the Fall: 'It was God who made the serpent and the woman and the man. And there wouldn't be an apple, if it wasn't in the plan. It's God they ought to crucify, instead of you and me, I said to the Carpenter, a-hanging on the tree.'

Ruether describes the potency of eucharistic sharing involving not only bread and wine: 'Women particularly need to claim and bless the symbol of the apple, since this innocent and good fruit has been absurdly turned into a symbol of evil and an assault against women as the source of evil. Thus a Eucharist of blessing and sharing the apple is particularly appropriate' (1985: 145). As the apple is blessed, these words are spoken: 'This is the apple of consciousness raising. Let the scales of false consciousness fall from our eyes, so that we can rightly name truth and falsehood, good and evil' (1985: 145). The reference is specifically to the role of the tree that stood in the middle of the garden, which was the tree of the knowledge of good and evil. While the Genesis story regards the desire for this knowledge as presumptuous and wicked, Ruether's blessing reinstates the desire for knowledge as well as the symbol of the apple. In a culture in which so much evil is disguised as good, and so much truth is untold, the knowledge of good and evil is essential to redress the balance. The blessing of the apple is a kind of truth telling in itself.

The figure of Mary is more complex, both in that we know more about her from Scripture—there is more to the story—and in that the various Christian traditions have treated her in such different ways. In my own radical Protestant tradition, Mary was really only part of the Christmas story. We learnt very little more about her than a somewhat sanitized and sentimental account of her part in the birth of Jesus. I have found it hard, therefore, but enriching to understand something of the devotion to Mary in the Roman Catholic traditions. Protestants find it easier to cope with the Orthodox notion of Mary as *theotokos*—the mother or bearer of God. At least, this way, she is still human.

There is, naturally, a vast resource of recent feminist liturgical writing about Mary. Her song, the Magnificat, has been reclaimed by liberation traditions of all kinds. New Christmas songs explore the relationship between Mary, the real mother, and Jesus as her child, from Sydney Carter's 'Come Love Carolling along in Me' to Judith Driver's 'Lullaby Baby'. No longer the cult figure, she can still be claimed as mother by feminist worshippers, for example, in June Boyce-Tillman's hymn, 'Mary our Mother'.

Thus, as Mary's story is interpreted by women's experience, and she becomes a fully human character in the Gospel narrative, her assumption of divine female imagery is exposed. Women must seek their imago not in Mary the mother of Jesus, but in God who created them in the image of God. This is, without question, the most controversial aspect of new worship material and the one which meets the full blast of misogyny, the hatred and the fear of women.

Female Imagery of God

Worship material which incorporates female imagery of God begins from Scripture, where there are—few, to be sure—female images of God. Brian Wren's litany of names for God, 'Glimpses of Holiness—Drawn from Scripture' (1997: 5-6), includes the midwife, mother eagle, mother and village woman. The passages in which God is imaged as a mother include the agony of giving birth and the care and comfort of a mother for her children. He omits the she-bear, savaging anyone who threatens her cubs, and Jesus' image of himself as a mother-hen.

In his hymns and in his book, *What Language Shall I Borrow* (Wren 1989) Wren explores the breadth of imagery from God, drawn from Scripture and from human life. In the hymn, 'Bring Many Names', the mother God is strong and creative, with some of the characteristics of Wisdom from the Wisdom writings, while the father God is warm and caring: not a capricious or polemical role reversal, but the reflection of biblical narrative and common human experience of mothers and fathers, if we are lucky. 'Who is She?' explores the life of Jesus as female, and sees God, 'dying to give birth, gasping yet exulting to a new creation'.

The motherhood of God has been explored in a variety of liturgical material. The resource which came out of the St Hilda Community contains a number of confessions of faith. Brenda Denvir's creed proclaims God as 'mother, source of deep wisdom', 'lover' and 'friend' (St Hilda Community 1991: 48). And two dramas from the Iona Community, the Drama of Creation and the Drama of the Incarnation, explore the same image (St Hilda Community 1991: 50).

Of course, female imagery of God is by no means a modern phenomenon. Some women writers are rediscovering and retranslating the works of the mediaeval women mystics who wrote and sang of God as female. Betty Wendelborn's 'O mother Jesus' is a translation from Julian of Norwich and uses an image, startling now, but not uncommon at the time, of Jesus lactating, providing milk from his 'breast' (the open side) which feeds and nourishes the believer who drinks from it. The hymn text is a prayer to Jesus, 'Oh mother Jesus, lead me to your breast/ to drink your nature, on your wisdom to feast', which Jesus answers, 'See how much I love you, of me you can feed,/ enter through my open side to take whatever you need' (Boyce-Tillman and Wootton 1993: no 27).

In 'After Eve', Janet Martin Soskice traces the use of female language about God and its gradual suppression through the first centuries of the Christian era (Soskice 1990). We are only just now rediscovering the feminine gender of the Spirit (*ruach*) in Hebrew. This would have been true of Jesus' speech, which was Aramaic, though the Greek word, (*pneuma*) is neuter. Brock's article (1990) looks at the treatment of the word in early literature of the Syriac-speaking church, where the word *ruḥa*, derived from the Hebrew word, is also feminine. She finds a gradual change of gender during the fifth and sixth centuries, from the grammatical feminine to the exclusive use of masculine.

But, more excitingly, many early texts use dramatic female imagery for all members of the Trinity. In the context of baptism and eucharist (Acts of Thomas, 27, 50, 133), God is referred to as 'compassionate mother' or 'hidden mother'. The Second Hymn of Synesios, Bishop of Cyrene in the early fifth century, contains the lines, 'I sing of the [Father's] travail, the fecund will, the intermediary principle, the Holy Breath/Inspiration, the centre point of the Parent, the centre point of the Child: she is sister, she is daughter; she has delivered [i.e. as midwife] the hidden root' (Brock 1990: 81).

The lactating God appears as early as the late second-century *Odes of Solomon*: 'A cup of milk was offered to me and I drank it in the sweetness of the Lord's kindness. The Son is the cup, and the Father is he who was milked and the Spirit is she who milked him. Because his breasts were full, and it was undesirable that his milk should be ineffectually released, the Holy Spirit opened her bosom, and mixed the milk of the two breasts of the Father' (Brock 1990: 83).

In the Middle Ages, the image appeared again, both in writing and in art. Bynum describes a complex of images of the nourishing of the believer. In some, the believer was being fed at the breast of the lactating virgin. In others, the believer was drinking from the blood of Christ, issuing from the wound in his side. The position of the wound and the attitude of the believer were clearly indicative of drinking milk from a breast. Clearly, the powerful involvement of women had an influence on the imagery and language of worship:

> [W]omen found it easy to identify with a deity whose flesh, like theirs, was food. In mystical ecstasy, in communion, in ascetic imitatio, women ate and became a God who was food and flesh. And in eating a God whose body was meat and drink, women both transfigured and became more fully the flesh and the food that their own bodies were' (Bynum 1987: 275).

In the Eastern tradition, the great female divine figure was Sophia, Wisdom, in whose name churches were dedicated and whose name suffuses the liturgy of the Church. This figure, again, is being rediscovered as a female image of God. Indeed, the Wisdom writings show her as assertively, aggressively female. She is God's playmate in the act of creation (Prov. 8.22-31). She sets up a holy brothel and sends her serving girls to call out, brazenly, on the street corners, touting for business (Prov. 9.1-6), rather different from the solemn splendid figure of Eastern liturgy.

Wisdom now re-enters the worshipping lives of feminist communities or radical churches, often identified with the incarnation of God, as in Jan Berry's hymn, 'Praise to God, the World's Creator', with its second verse beginning, 'Praise to God, our saving Wisdom/Meeting us with love and grace'. My own round, 'By your shaping, by your wisdom and delight, we are crafted in your image, deep loving God', seeks to interweave creation accounts, using male and female imagery of creation, to undergird the imago Dei for women as well as men.

In her hymn, 'It Was Dark in the Dawn of Time', June Boyce-Tillman makes a further link with the creativity of human beings in giving birth: 'It is dark in the sheltering womb/Where the baby for nine months lies,/Curved like a moon near a warm woman's heart/Till the waters roll aside'; and in intellectual activity: 'It is dark in the heart's deep cells/Where the Spirit of Wisdom lies./Firm are the strong rooms and bars of the mind/Till the barriers are rolled aside.' Each verse ends with the line, 'As the Spirit worked (works) out her plan'.

Much of this material arouses intense hostility. My own hymn, 'Dear Mother God', travels from the mother eagle of Deuteronomy 32 to the exultant eagle of Isaiah 40. This hymn has aroused extraordinary vilification, even though it is thoroughly and specifically scripturally based, a fact which has made it acceptable to others. One of the great pioneers in the development of radical material for worship, Janet Morley, has experienced the ritual burning of her books. And yet mainstream hymnbooks and liturgical resources in some parts of the world are beginning to accept hymns with female imagery of God. Perhaps there is hope.

Women in Scripture and Tradition

We are also rediscovering the wealth of women's stories in Scripture and tradition. From the Hebrew Scriptures, Sarah, Miriam and Deborah are well enough known figures to have attracted liturgical writing. In particular, they are seen as role models for strength and joy in women's lives. All three played an important part in the leadership of the people of God in their time. Each has been overshadowed by powerful men in their own narratives: Sarah needs to be reclaimed in liturgical material which concentrates on Abraham; Miriam is almost unknown in traditional material beside her brother Moses, and even Aaron; Deborah is not overshadowed by the male characters in her own story (Barak or Sisera); instead, her story fades in the background of stories about other judges—Gideon, Samson and, of course, Samuel.

There is a great deal of room for creative encounter with other women from these scriptures. Hagar is as hidden by Sarah as Sarah is by Abraham. There is room to celebrate the Hebrew midwives who saved the new-born babies of the Israelites, Hannah and her co-wife, Penninah, indeed, all those women who were wives and concubines whose happiness or despair turned on their fertility (or the fertility of their husband/owner, since failure to conceive was always blamed on the woman). The story of Ruth and Naomi has enormous scope for interpretative writing. There are many others.

Some are remembered in the liturgical material which grew out of the St Hilda Community and its successors. Janet Morley celebrates Ruth in the collect, 'God of the Outsider' (St Hilda Community 1991: 43), in which Ruth's position as grandmother of King David, and her boldness in claiming the right to life are honoured. A confession drawn from a World Council of Churches publication uses Eve, Miriam, Deborah, Naomi and Ruth, Mary, Thecla and Phoebe as exemplars whose pattern we have failed to follow (St Hilda Community 1991: 58). And a lovely blessing by Lois M. Wilson recalls Sarah and Hagar, as well as Abraham (St Hilda Community 1991: 80).

Celebrating Women (Morley and Ward 1986), is a great repository of the creativity of women's liturgical writing. Images of God as mother, lover, dancer, and stirrer of life leap from the pages. Women and their lives are celebrated with vigour and anger. Janet Crawford's and Erice Webb's 'A Litany for Many Voices' speaks in the name of Eve, Sarah, Miriam, Delilah, of Jepthah's daughter, of Jezebel ('trampled by horses, eaten by dogs, but I painted my eyes and adorned my head and met death wearing my crown'), of Vashti, Judith, Ruth, Naomi, Anna and many New Testament women. The litany ends with Mary, who says, 'I loved my baby for which eternally I must wear the patriarchal crown. I beseech you, my sisters, help me remove the weight and lay it down' (Morley and Ward 1986: 12).

In the New Testament, almost none of the women who followed Jesus, or held positions of leadership in the early churches, is sung in the liturgical traditions. Mary, the mother of Jesus, appears at Christmas and Easter in the Protestant churches and more widely in the Roman Catholic and Orthodox traditions. But even the women at the tomb are strangely absent from the worshipping life of most churches. One difficulty is that a great many of the women who encountered Jesus are anonymous in Scripture. In liturgical material, their mention needs to be descriptive rather than by name.

The Samaritan woman who met Jesus at the well had a theological discussion with him which may well have influenced his thinking about the kind of mission he had to perform (see Jn 4.35-38 in the light of the conversation recorded in the first half of that chapter). She also becomes for us an example of the independent, strong woman, unafraid to live unconventionally and possessed of a tough intelligence which it must have been very difficult to exercise in her culture and circumstances. The Syro-Phoenician woman who challenged Jesus' thinking about inclusivity, the woman who anointed Jesus' head and the woman who poured perfume over his feet touch our experience in different ways.

It is no longer enough simply to mention these women. While it is undoubtedly important that their stories are told and heard again, liturgists must listen to and work with theologians, so that the full impact of these women's actions and words is made known. Because we lack a tradition of writing about the women of Scripture, the theology of their stories has not been developed through the ages. Compared with, say, the theology of the stories of the male disciples, told and retold through liturgy and song, the stories of the women of Scripture have a long way to go.

For example, the women at the tomb were constant—they 'stood by' Jesus—and this is honoured in a collect by Monica Furlong in which Jesus is asked to 'stand by us in the darkness of our crucifixions' in the same way (St Hilda Community 1991: 43). They were also not believed. Their experience of the divine was despised, as is the religious experience of women throughout the ages. Janet Morley's collect, 'O God, the Power of the Powerless' (St Hilda Community 1991: 43) recognizes this, as does Fred Pratt Green's satirical hymn, 'What Tale Is This our Women Bring?' The chorus, 'Hurry, hurry brothers; do not more delay./ Maybe it is true what the women say', and the verse, 'Let brother Peter, brother John,/ Whose word we can rely upon,/ Seek out the truth...', describe the scepticism of the male disciples. The last verse echoes the frustration of women: 'We women who still long to share/ The good news that dispels despair...' (Women in Theology 1988: 7).

That hymn was sung at the service to launch the World Council of Churches Decade for the Churches in Solidarity with Women at Westminster Abbey on Low Sunday of 1988. The men were invited to sing the sceptical verses, with the women joining in the chorus.

Brian Wren's hymn, 'Woman in the Night', attempts to portray the power of some of the women, named and unnamed, who encountered Jesus: 'Woman at the well,/Question the Messiah;/Find your friends and tell;/Drink your heart's desire. Woman in the house,/Nurtured to be meek,/Leave your second place;/Listen, think, and speak!' June Boyce-Tillman's hymn about Mary at the tomb focuses on her desire to stay close to Jesus, to 'cling', and recognizes the call for women like her to balance the ecstasy of contemplation with the requirement to bring about change: 'She recognised her love/Who told her not to stay;/so she left her contemplation/For the world of everyday. At times, God,

you seem close,/But help us not to cling,/May such ecstasy be har-
nessed/For the world's transfiguring.'

The women of the early church are honoured in the St Hilda liturgies. Phoebe and Thecla have already been mentioned. A eucharistic
prayer also includes the company of saints, with whom we praise God,
'all those who inspired and supported the early Church... Tabitha who
showed solidarity with the poor, Lydia who welcomed the tired and
travel weary and Priscilla who knew the meaning of persecution' (St
Hilda Community 1991: 66).

The eucharist itself ought to be a place for celebrating women's stories. Women are the makers and providers of food. Women's bodies and
blood are the nourishers of new life. Far from the violent symbolism of
sacrifice, and authoritarian restrictions based on appropriateness and
purity, women's approaches to eucharist have been freeing, celebratory
and inclusive. Frances Croake Frank's 'Did the Woman Say?' throws
into shocking opposition Mary's right to say of Jesus at his birth and his
death, 'This is my body; this is my blood', and the refusal of the Church
to allow women to say those words in consecration of the eucharist:
'Well that she said it to him then. For dry old men, Brocaded robes
belying barrenness, Ordain that she not say it for him now' (Morley and
Ward 1986: 38).

Many feminist eucharistic liturgies recognize women's part in the
provision of the elements, imaging God whom Jesus pictures as the
woman baking (Mt. 13.33). In recognition of the mundanity of the
elements, and their appropriateness both to nourishing and to feasting,
women's eucharistic liturgies have called on the imagery of the wedding
at Cana (Jn 2), and the great harvest festivals of the Hebrew Scriptures.
Often, the bread which is used has been baked for the eucharist by
members of the community which celebrates it.

Celebration of the great feast carries the theology of inclusion. In the
parables of the feast, the rich and powerful exclude themselves, while
the servants are sent again and again into the streets to bring in the poor,
those whose lives are blighted—everyone whose presence is totally
unexpected at the rich royal banquet. Megan McKenna begins her book
about the neglected stories in the Bible (1994), with the image of who is
left out of the feeding miracles and teachings of Jesus. The answer is that
none is excluded by Jesus. The *Church* has been systematically excluding
people for centuries.

She describes a ritual using oranges, in which participants feed segments to each other as signs of words from Scripture which have a powerful meaning for the person who is doing the feeding in relation to the person being fed. The 'celebrant' picks up the leftovers and feeds others as they find meaning. Occasionally someone thinks to feed the celebrant, though, McKenna notes, this does not always happen. The ritual challenges the participants to be fed by others, and to join in a symbol of sharing, of inclusion (1994: 30-32).

By taking seriously the inclusive nature of eucharistic sharing, worshippers make a prophetic statement, heralding the community of promise. It is, writes M. Shawn Copeland, 'a mere routine of *pro forma* act, if we have not confessed our sins, repented of our participation and/or collusion in the marginalisation of others; if we have not begged forgiveness from those who we have offended; if we have not pledged firm purpose of amendment; if we have not moved to healing and creative Christian praxis' (1994: 30).

Besides Scripture, there is a whole hidden history of women to be sung. Christians in certain traditions are accustomed to hymns and prayers based on the lives of saints. Two recent trends have opened the way to the veneration of people not officially sanctified by the Church. First, there is a desire to celebrate people recognized as great by our own era, but whose names would not be likely to appear on any official list of saints. So there is a Martin Luther King day now, celebrated in the calendar of many churches. The newly restored west front of Westminster Abbey has statues of twentieth-century martyrs. Among them are well-known martyrs such as Dietrich Bonhoeffer, Martin Luther King and Oscar Romero. But there are also less well-known women: Manche Masemola, killed in South Africa in 1928 by her animist parents, and Esther John, killed in Pakistan in 1960, allegedly by a Muslim fanatic.

Alongside this trend has been the desire to see women specifically celebrated for their achievements. Among these may be saints, but their lives are celebrated now in terms of their actions and words, rather than their martyrdom or purity. Others have never been, nor are likely to be, sanctified.

Of course, the great names of mediaeval women mystics and religious are there. Hildegard of Bingen is at the heart of a great revival in the singing of early chant. Her rich, poetic imagery finds immediate resonances with feminist theological thought. God is 'breath' and 'air' on which we float like feathers. Her concept of 'viriditas'—'greening', or the power of fecundity in the created world—finds certain parallels in eco-feminism, and the sense in feminist liturgy of wholeness with creation.

Julian of Norwich is also widely represented in recent feminist liturgical writing. She wrote graphically of Jesus as Mother, as quoted on p. 41. The image of the world as an object the size of a walnut, held in the palm, is again concurrent with the feminist sense of oneness with the world.

At the conference in Durham, in 1998 at the end of the World Council of Churches Decade, the Churches in Solidarity with Women, women of the four nations (England, Ireland, Scotland, Wales) were invited to bring the names of women from their own traditions to celebrate. The woman who was celebrated for the British Isles was St Hilda. Her icon had been painted by Edith Reyntiens, a Russian Orthodox icon painter in the authentic tradition. The central panel shows Hilda standing with a scroll in her left hand, her right hand extended in blessing, while the surrounding vignettes tell the story of her life. Her icon was dedicated by a (male, of course) Roman Catholic priest in the context of the communion service, conducted by women of Anglican, Roman Catholic and Free Church traditions.

Of course, Hildegard, Julian and others are flawed 'feminist heroes'. How could they embody twentieth- or twenty-first-century feminist principles in a culture that was entirely different? That is not to say that we ignore their writings or that their stories are not worth telling. Unlike sanctification, celebration does not require the attainment of perfection (even through martyrdom).

Here, again, there is room for expanding the field. Because of the dominance of the Roman Catholic tradition in Europe and the Anglican tradition (which is broadly catholic) in England, names of women outside these traditions are not celebrated. The lives and achievements of the great women of the Reformation, and of the early independent traditions are unknown, but their lives were often fulfilling and exciting, and they were breaking new ground in women's leadership.

At Durham, not all the women celebrated were saints. The Welsh nominated Ann Griffiths (1776–1805), a hymnwriter whose hymns are no longer very much sung, but who certainly had a powerful influence on hymnwriting. It is, perhaps, in the area of hymnwriting that the contribution of women has been most scandalously treated. Throughout the history of hymnody in the English-speaking traditions—that is, in the last 300 years—there have been many and prolific women writers.

Anne Laetitia Barbauld (born Anne Aikin, 1743–1825) is another early writer, this time from the Unitarian tradition, whose hymns are now hardly ever sung. She was a radical political writer, who, under a variety of male pseudonyms, trenchantly satirized the warlike pomp of her day, and wrote in support of the abolition of slavery. Her satire on a prayer for God's help in battle shows a healthy contempt for state religion:

> God of love, father of all the families of the earth, we are going to tear in pieces our brethren of mankind, but our strength is not equal to our fury, we beseech thee to assist us in the work of slaughter... Whatever mischief we do, we shall do it in thy name; we hope, therefore, thou wilt protect us in it. Thou, who hast made of one blood all the dwellers upon the earth, we trust thou wilt view us alone with partial favour, and enable us to bring misery upon every other quarter of the globe' (Barbauld 1793: 403-404)

This she based on the principle that 'an unjust war is in itself so bad a thing, that there is only one way of making it worse, and that is, by mixing religion with it'. (Barbauld 1793: 405)

Barbauld also wrote a series of prose hymns for children (1781), considering poetry to be too sophisticated and distracting for young minds. As with her political writing, her devotional texts are occasionally startlingly radical. Her 'Hymn III' includes a stanza comparing God to the human mother known to the child:

> The mother loveth her little child; she bringeth it up on her knees; she nourisheth its body with food; she feedeth its mind with knowledge; if it is sick, she nurseth it with tender love; she watcheth over it when asleep; she forgetteth it not for a moment; she teacheth it how to be good; she rejoiceth daily in its growth.
>
> But who is the parent of the mother? who nourisheth her with good things, and watcheth over her with tender love, and remembereth her every moment? Whose arms are about her to guard her from harm? and if she is sick, who shall heal her.
>
> God is the parent of the mother; he is the parent of all, for he created all. All the men and all the women who are alive in the wide world are his children; he loveth all, he is good to all (Barbauld 1781: 14-16).

'Hymn V' is all about sleeping, and contains the lovely stanza:

> As the mother moveth about the house with her finger on her lips, and stilleth every little noise, that her infant be not disturbed; as she draweth the curtains around its bed, and shutteth out the light from its tender eyes; so God draweth the darkness around us, so he maketh all things to be hushed and still, that his large family may sleep in peace.

Barbauld's hymns may not be sung now, but her influence on the next generation was enormous. Harriet Martineau, a prominent writer in support of women's full participation in society, records her own indebtedness to Barbauld; a generation of Unitarian writers were brought up on her hymns, in particular, Sarah Flower Adams (1805–1848), daughter of a prominent social reformer, jailed for supporting the French Revolution. Never mind what may or may not have been sung on the *Titanic*, Sarah Flower Adams's intense and scriptural hymn, 'Nearer my God to Thee', deserves to be known more widely.

In America, the Unitarian tradition produced Love Maria Willis (1824–1908), writer of 'Father, Hear the Prayer we Offer', which, despite the exclusive terminology of its first line, is valuable as a call to strenuous effort, in opposition to the quietism which is generally considered to be characteristic of women's writing. Her hymns reflect the gathering tension during the years leading up to the American Civil War. Writing at the same time, but better known for her prose writing than her hymns, Harriet Beecher Stowe (1811–96) also reflects the strong social conscience of these years. The hymn, 'Mine Eyes Have Seen the Glory of the Coming of the Lord', by Julia Ward Howe (1819–1910), refers very directly to the War, using the tune of 'John Brown's Body', more commonly sung to lyrics designed to stir up partisan hatred, but instead making the words a rallying call to a new world.

In the Church of England, women writers were drawn up along theological battlelines. In the nineteenth century, Evangelical and Catholic constituencies produced worship material in support of their own theology. On one side, for example, there was Frances Ridley Havergal (1836–79), a brilliant and accomplished young woman, who could have had a considerable social career by the standards of her day. However, after a religious experience, she chose to put her talents to the enrichment of worship. She was a fervent evangelical and wrote hymns of intense personal devotion: 'Take My Life and Let It Be Consecrated, Lord, to Thee'; 'Lord Speak to Me that I May Speak in Living Echoes of thy Tone'.

Another passionate evangelical was Christina Rossetti (1830–94), who set out to bring the devotional wealth of German hymnody to English-speaking congregations. She translated many well-known and loved Christmas hymns, including 'In the Bleak Midwinter' and 'Love Came Down at Christmas'.

On the other side, the hymns of Claudia Frances Hernaman (1836–

79) are avowedly Anglo-Catholic. She was co-editor of *The Altar Hymnal* (1884) a deliberate attempt to gather hymnody which reflected the sacraments and the doctrine of the Church. Better known is Cecil Frances Alexander (1818–95), whose writing for children was intended to teach the doctrines of the creed in terms that they could understand. Her best known hymns, 'All Things Bright and Beautiful', 'There Is a Green Hill Far Away' and 'Once in Royal David's City', are still extremely popular.

Some women hymnwriters from the Anglican tradition were also involved in working for the rights of women. Catherine Winkworth (1827–78) was a pioneer in higher education for women. She founded Clifton High School for Girls and attended conferences in support of women's education. And Dora Greenwell (1821–82) belonged to a group of radical thinkers and writers, including Josephine Grey (later Butler), who exposed the 'double standard' employed in legislation about prostitution.

Greenwell's writing is far less 'certain' than that of either Evangelical or Anglo-Catholic camps. Her lovely hymn of the incarnation, 'And Art thou Come with Us to Dwell', uses haunting imagery of paradise to describe the realized eschatology of the incarnation. The poetry echoes the fluid nature of the imagery, with caesurae at various places in the lines, and many thoughts extending over the line ends: 'Thou bringest all again; with Thee/ Is light, is space, is breadth and room/ For each thing fair, beloved and free/ To have its hour of life and bloom. Each heart's deep instinct unconfessed;/ Each lowly wish, each daring claim;/ All, all that life has long repressed/ Unfolds, undreading blight or blame.'

At the same time, the Evangelical revival saw the enormously prolific Frances Jane Van Alstyne (1820–1915), who is said to have written over 8,000 hymns. She wrote under a series of pseudonyms, the most well-known being her maiden name, Fanny Crosby. Among her enormous output are several still well-loved hymns: 'Blessed Assurance, Jesus Is Mine', 'To God Be the Glory', 'All the Way my Saviour Leads Me', 'Jesus Keep Me near the Cross'.

Despite their presence in practically every hymnwriting tradition, and the fact that their hymns are inextricably interwoven in the best-known and best-loved 'core' of congregational singing, women hymnwriters are frequently regarded as a separate species. Books on hymnwriting will trace the history of writing entirely from a male perspective, with a

chapter at the end on women writers. This must entail the careful exci-
sion of women writers from history, but it is the norm in books written
most of the way through the twentieth century.

During the early years of the twentieth century, women's hymnwriting was mainly for children—not that that is by any means an easy
field. The 1960s folk revival was spearheaded by male writers such as
Sydney Carter, Peter Smith and Geoffrey Ainger. Their writing broke
new ground in terms of the recognition of social issues, the unity of
humankind, and so on, but the language was uncompromisingly male. I
may have, 'a sister in Melbourne, a brother in Paree' but I belong to,
'The family of man', which, 'keeps growing…keeps sowing the seed of
a new life every day'.

It was not until the 1970s and 1980s that the language even of well-
intentioned social worship was challenged and women began to be consciously celebrated in hymns. At its mildest, this shows itself in re-writes
and new hymns in which 'brothers' become 'sisters and brothers'.
Ironically, the ease of rhyming 'brother' works to the advantage of
inclusive language in putting 'sisters' first, which is not the traditional
order in the English language and, like 'women and men', gives pause
for thought.

Some individual women's lives are celebrated. Elizabeth Cosnett's
hymn, 'For God's Sake Let Us Dare/To pray like Josephine' focuses on
the life of Josephine Butler, the great campaigner for the rights of prosti-
tutes. Cosnett's hymn bluntly faces the issue raised: 'She forced her age
to face/ What most it feared to see,/ The double standards at the base/
Of its prosperity.' The message of Josephine Butler and her tough spirituality are there in the hymn. She has now been incorporated into the
Anglican liturgical calendar.

Cecily Taylor writes about Elizabeth Fry. 'There Are Times I Still
Dream of the Nightmare at Newgate' a swinging sea shanty, describes
the despair of women transported to 'Botany Bay', and the hope
brought by the gift Elizabeth ensured was given to each one.

In October 1997 we celebrated 80 years of women's ordination in
Britain. This was a difficult concept. We focused on Constance
Coltman, who was ordained into the ministry of a congregational
church in 1917. Of course, women had been in leadership positions in
the Religious Society of Friends and the Salvation Army for years before
1917 and Gertrude von Petzholt was ordained to a Unitarian church in
1916, and so, many argued, we ought to have celebrated her. We did

include a serving Unitarian woman minister in the leadership of the service.

Celebrating 80 years of women's ordination was partly, at least, an antidote to the failure of the English generally and the press in particular to acknowledge any ordained women in England before 1994. People are still astounded to know that women were ordained so long ago. The leader of the service, and one of the story-tellers, was Revd Florence Frost Mee, ordained in 1951.

As we were honouring Constance, I wrote a hymn in her honour, setting her in the tradition of Miriam, who danced the first dance of freedom on the shores of the Red Sea, and Mary the first apostle from the empty tomb. The verse about Constance honours her fierce integrity and passion for justice: 'With Constance we will stand/For what we know is right/In answer to God's just demand/And searching sight./Confronting each abuse/That strangles liberty,/God help us simply speak the truth/That sets us free.' The tune to which the words were written was 'Leoni', more commonly sung to the words, 'The God of Abraham praise'. This impressive and very male hymn forms the background to some of the words, so that the singer may enter into dialogue with the tradition. So, for example, the last verse, 'Made whole, the human race/ May answer to God's call', deliberately echoes the last verse of the traditional words, 'The whole triumphant host/ Give thanks to God on high', bringing the triumphant transcendence of traditional worship into contrast with the presence of God in the renewed human community which is the emphasis of so much feminist writing. Since then, Marlene Phillips, a woman composer, has written another tune to the words, so the association is lost—but the new tune is lovely!

There are other communities of women whose experience appears in recent hymnwriting. The late twentieth century, like its earlier years, has been a time of shifting populations, of refugees from war, driven from their homelands, of fugitives from oppressive regimes and of people simply seeking a better life. Lois Ainger's dramatic hymn, 'We Know the Songs of Zion from our Youth', traces the experience of refugees, their vulnerability and their sadness as the next generation loses language and culture and is absorbed into the host population—another kind of oppression. The chorus echoes Ps. 137.1, 2, 6: 'By the rivers of Babylon we listen and remember. We hang our harps on the willow tree and the music of our grief is in the silence.' Many refugees are women. Of refugee communities, often the most oppressed are women, and they are also likely to be the carriers of their culture, and so grieve most heartily to see it disappear.

There are two other great traditions of these years which have provided a context for women's writing. One is the Iona Community, whose leading lights have been John Bell and Graham Maule; however, Anna Briggs and Kathy Galloway are sensitive and thoughtful writers from the group. Kathy Galloway's hymn, 'She Comes with a Mother's Kindness', is included in the recent Scottish ecumenical collection, *Common Ground* (1998). Although the hymn does not refer directly to the Holy Spirit, but uses the language that Scripture uses to speak more generally of God, the note to the hymn links it with the Spirit: 'It may seem unusual in one collection to have two hymns which allude to the Holy Spirit in the feminine. This is not to say that the Spirit is a woman, but to encourage deeper thinking about the nature and work of the Spirit.' It is a shame that, in a collection which will be used by congregations and therefore publicly and widely available, such a lovely text should be tied to a negative and limiting note. Anna Briggs's 'We Lay our Broken World' is also included.

Another extremely creative area of liturgical writing is Aotearoa New Zealand. The churches are consciously attempting to develop a bi-cultural stance, that is, indigenous and incoming peoples working together. This openness shows itself further in the development of a very inclusive hymnody. The hymnbook *Alleluia Aotearoa* (1992), contains liturgical material in a number of Polynesian languages as well as in English. Cecily Sheehy's 'Colour Me Free', a fun song with shouted verses, celebrates 'the colours we be!/When we're together, what a beautiful sight—/different shades of brown and lots of black and white'. Shirley Murray tackles the liturgical presence of people with disabilities quite directly in, 'Who Is my Mother?', in the verse, 'Differently abled,/ differently labelled/ widen the circle round Jesus Christ,/ crutches and stigmas,/ cultures enigmas/ all come together round Jesus Christ.'

This is a book alive with female imagery of God, a celebratory inclusiveness of all God's people, a lively concern for the environments in which we live, city and country. There is even an 'upside down Christmas', which pokes fun at the anomaly of northern Christmas imagery in the Southern Hemisphere.

The hymnbook published for the middle of the Decade, *Reflecting Praise* (Boyce-Tillman and Wootton 1993) gathers much of the inclusive material that was around at the time. It begins with 'Dear Mother

God', and ends with the hymn that shows signs of becoming the rallying cry of those who wish to release the silenced voices. Although it does not specifically mention women, and is therefore open to all repressed communities, it was written with the silencing of women in mind, and I quote it in full:

> We shall go out with hope of resurrection,
> We shall go out, from strength to strength go on,
> We shall go out and tell our stories boldly,
> Tales of a love that will not let us go.
> We'll sing our songs of wrongs that can be righted,
> We'll dream our dreams of hurts that can be healed,
> We'll weave a cloth of all the world united
> Within the vision of a Christ who sets us free.
>
> We'll give a voice to those who have not spoken,
> We'll find the words for those whose lips are sealed,
> We'll make the tunes for those who sing no longer,
> Vibrating love alive in every heart.
> We'll share our joy with those who are still weeping,
> Chant hymns of strength for hearts that break in grief,
> We'll leap and dance the resurrection story
> Including all within the circles of our love.[1]

The Shape of Space for Worship

With this emphasis on inclusiveness and equality, the 'shape' of feminist liturgy has favoured a flat, circular seating arrangement, rather than lengthways seating with a dais or stage at one end for the leaders. In fact, this, like other elements of feminist worship, marks the rediscovery of a feature which is characteristic of women's participation in leadership.

It is also part of a more general trend. With recent changes in styles of worship, with the emphasis in the liturgical traditions shifting from priest to priest and people, and the emphasis in the preaching churches shifting from preacher to preacher and congregation, church architecture has undergone several alterations. Altars have moved west, to be nearer the crossing and, consequently, the people. Large pulpits stand empty in non-conformist Victorian churches, while the worship leader often prefers to conduct the service from the same level as the congregation.

The principle is articulated in the architecture inspired by a group of

1.   'We Shall Go Out', June Boyce-Tillman. ©1993 Stainer & Bell Ltd, London and Women in Theology from *Reflecting Praise*. Used with permission.

Unitarian women ministers and church leaders who took on churches in
the frontier towns in the American West in the nineteenth century.
There, church architecture reflected a way of defining the relationship
between the preacher and the people. In the Western churches, simplicity of form was perhaps enforced by the pioneering nature of the
work. However, there is evidence that the women preferred a lower
pulpit, bringing the preacher down to the same level as the congregation, and a less ornate church building. Tucker writes:

> Religiously liberal women had both theological and feminist reasons for
> shunning the traditional Gothic design. As a minister's wife pointed out,
> what a congregation believed and how it behaved were 'unconsciously
> moulded' by a sanctuary's physical properties... The distaff's advocacy of
> a less aristocratic idiom was also a way of promoting a devotional lan-
> guage that better expressed the egalitarian ideal on which their liberal
> movement was founded. The stately Gothic cathedrals in which the East's
> most conservative liberal men preached had become for the women visi-
> ble statements of patriarchal resistance to their equal access to leadership
> in the church (1994: 107).

There is a precedent to this in the writings of Anna Laetitia Barbauld.
She foresaw a time when an equalizing form of worship would result in
buildings which were 'amphitheatrical in form', rather than, 'those little
gloomy solitary cells, planned by the spirit of aristocracy, which...favour
at once the pride of rank and the laziness of indulgence' (Barbauld 1792:
459). This is because 'It is of service to the cause of freedom...no less
than to that of virtue, that there is one place where the invidious
distinctions of wealth and titles are not admitted; where all are equal, not
by making the low, proud, but by making the great, humble' (Barbauld
1792: 446) and 'Every time Social Worship is celebrated, it includes a
virtual declaration of the rights of man [sic]' (Barbauld 1792: 448). This
is in contrast to her view of what she might have called patriarchal
worship in which 'men have imagined to themselves how a Nero or
Domitian would have acted, if, from the extent of their dominion there
had been no escape, and to the duration of it no period' (Barbauld 1792:
465) and based their view of God on that ultimate despotism.

Union Chapel was built in the nineteenth century, consciously using
the same kinds of principles as those outlined by Barbauld, has been
further adapted for use by a twentieth-century congregation.

This magnificent Victorian preaching 'box' is built on the principle
that every member of the 2000-strong congregation should be able to
see and hear the preacher. The pews form a semi-circular shape beneath

a high dome. One child who visited recently described it as 'like being inside an egg'. All the emphasis is on participation. There are no choir stalls, since it was considered the duty of every member of the congregation to participate in the praises of God. Choirs were seen as 'vicarious worship' on the part of a congregation which should be taking its own priestly responsibility seriously. To this end, by the way, full congregational singing practices were held weekly, and the church, in its Victorian heyday, was capable of singing the 'Hallelujah Chorus' from Handel's *Messiah* as part of its regular worship.

Clyde Binfield writes, 'Wherever you sit in an octagonal building you are its central point. In this respect Union is a very Protestant, a very individualising, space. This place for listeners to Word (or music) is no place for those who prefer the sidelines, for the moment you are seated in it you are on the preacher's sight-line.' He goes on, 'And if you are in an ecclesiastical frame of mind, then you might reflect that from the tower gallery the whole church space has become a chancel.' The chancel was the priests' part of the medieval church, but in a Protestant church all are priests. So Union's architect has not just got his Gothic right, he has adapted it with rare subtlety (Wootton 1999: 6).

The situation was not perfect, of course. The marble dais with its imposing communion table, and the 10-foot pulpit still placed the preacher in a highly elevated position. And while there is very little differentiation in seating, we know that, in fact, people were seated by social rank, with the 'carriage trade' seated in the central block of pews, lower classes perhaps at the sides, and the servants, shop boys, and so on, in the gallery.

The now much smaller congregation can make use of the huge space delightfully creatively. There is a pewless space (courtesy of alterations in the 1970s) at the back, which provides plenty of room for dance, or other informal gatherings. It is also sometimes possible to gather the whole congregation on the stage for communion round the table, rather than from it. The magnificent pulpit now forms the dramatic background to worship at ground-floor level. We feel as though we are developing, rather than having to counteract the theological impulses of those who designed the building.

Egalitarian use can also be made of a longways-style church. Peggy Jackson was among the first women to be ordained into the Church of England. She was ordained at St Albans Abbey, which is—as she says— long and vast. She and the others who were planning the service made the decision to use the shape of the Abbey in a symbolic way. She writes

> The long procession of entrance came in at the South Transept, turned
> East, to enter the shrine of St. Alban behind the High Altar at the East
> End. It then moved the length of the choir into the nave, where the
> ordinations took place. This took a long time, with the congregation
> singing, and the ordinands acting out the long journey of the women and
> the whole Church of England to this moment. People remarked on the
> astounding circumstance that the procession was 'beaming', and everyone
> was smiling. There was a lot of room for weeping as well as singing, and
> there was space for weeping and applause during the Peace and at the
> ordinations (Jackson 1994: 21-22).

The ordinations took place at the nave altar, with the closest guests sitting in the nave where they could see. Communion was celebrated at the crossing, which more or less everyone could see, and was distributed at various points in the Abbey. In a building of traditional shape, the point of inertia is traditional style liturgies. Peggy notes the amount of planning and commitment in the face of pressure to conform which was required to ensure that the worship on this occasion was as innovative and effective as it was.

Rosemary Radford Ruether describes what a whole purpose-built complex for worship of this kind would be like (1985: 146). The space would need to be both centring and elevating. She describes a circular space with a dome to let in natural light, and oriented to catch light at both winter and summer solstices. Under the celebration centre, there would be a crypt for rituals connected with birth and death. The whole complex would consist of the celebration centre, an egg-shaped building for study or conversation, gardens, pools, saunas, a play-centre, places for weaving, pottery and other crafts, a library, and cottages where people could stay.

As well as shape, iconography is fundamentally important. Stained-glass windows filled with representations of socially powerful male figures, or male characters from Scripture, are very difficult to counter with female imagery and language in worship. Even where modern stained glass exists, it is often male oriented. In Southwark Cathedral, the windows depict work being done. This, importantly, brings the lives of ordinary people into the imagery which informs the worshipping space, not the rich and powerful who have the money to give large donations to the church. Unfortunately, of course, the artisans shown at work are male. The iconography is of strong men in the public sphere.

The Orthodox churches have great gifts of iconography to offer.

With a theology of icons that links their use as imagery with the imaging of God in human beings, this tradition offers a great many female images. These are not just pictures of women, but provide the means to honour their stories and achievements, and to construct them as role models for the worshipping community. The painter of the St Hilda icon which was dedicated at the Durham conference, Edith Reyntiens, explained to us the ways in which we could approach the icon in worship, to release its capacity to enrich our lives and to give us the strength shown by the saint whose life it describes. The icon is now lodged in Durham Cathedral, and we pray that it will enrich and strengthen the lives of worshippers and visitors.

I would argue that, in this sense of iconography, other objects may perform an iconographic function in worship. Banners, tapestries and sculptures may become bearers of meaning for a congregation. To be iconographic, I would suggest that images or symbols should have the power to demonstrate the image of God in the lives of human beings, and that they should be effective in empowering worshippers. I would also suggest that images should have some endurance beyond the individual act of worship, and beyond the community which is gathered on that occasion. If, say, a worship leader decides to use the imagery of balloons bursting to indicate determination to puncture the pomposity of destructive powers, that is a piece of imagery. Even if he or she thinks this is such a good idea that he or she uses it over and over again in different contexts, it is still imagery, and potentially very effective, but not iconographic.

Icons carry the story of a community through time. To this effect, it is the actual fabric that is important. *This* tapestry which was woven in *this* context is the purveyor of meaning. A copy does not have the same effect.

Examples of this kind of work are the many quilts which have been made by communities of women to express their hope and pain. The 'Durham quilt', put together for a celebration of European Christian women in 1992, has travelled all over the world. Local churches and other groups were invited to create squares celebrating women and to provide a short biography of the women they had chosen.

The women whose lives are celebrated span the centuries. They include writers, social reformers, missionaries, church leaders, academics, broadcasters, homemakers, even an astronaut. The squares are made in a great variety of styles and the impression of the whole quilt is overwhelming. As such it is truly iconic, since its very presence—the fact that this is the Durham quilt, which women's hands have made—carries the message of hope and power. The stories are told in an illustrated book edited by Lavinia Byrne and published by the Council of Churches for Britain and Ireland (*Christian Women Together*, CCBI 1992).

Christian Survivors of Sexual Abuse have also made a quilt, telling their own experience of pain and despair. This is heartrending to see. It is the frontispiece to silence and terrible compassion. Again, it is the quilt itself that is important, its objectivity telling the subjective horror of the women whose hands, sometimes bearing the scars of self-mutilation, have created the images. A copy or a picture of the quilt is powerful, but it is not the same as the presence of the thing itself.

From a similar community within the Baptist churches has come a set of T-shirts, painted and embroidered by women survivors of abuse. At the Durham conference, these were displayed on the stairs leading from the conference hall to the dining area. Elsewhere they have been used in worship, and shown at national functions. Even out of the context of worship, their power is intense. The onlooker cannot escape the cry that echoes from image after image along the long line of suffering.

Other icons can be created over a shorter time span. At a gathering over several days, a community may bring elements from workshops or from the lives of the participants into worship day by day. I would argue that these have the capacity to become icons, even though they may not outlast the conference or gathering at which they are made. One way of enabling this is to string a series of parallel threads which will become the warp into which participants can weave their weft from colours and objects which reflect their experience during the time together. This will develop over a series of acts of worship and will come to embody something of the life of that community over a short period of time. As well as feelings of awe and solidarity, images of this kind can arouse intense hostility. This is true of the figures of women on the cross which have emerged from various communities.

Incidentally, this is very different from the iconography of the entrance to the new British Library, in which much of the research for this book was carried out. The new building is monumental in scale, the approach being consciously hieratic, as the reader passes through the profanum of the courtyard into the liminal area, a full-height entrance hall, with the huge edifice of the Kings Library concealing the holy space beyond. Only a few sacred pathways—stairs and escalators guarded by automatic ticket barriers—indicate the way from the great hall to the truly sacred space, which only initiates can access.

On the way, the reader passes a number of statues. In the courtyard is a massive sculpture of 'Newton after William Blake' by Eduardo Paolozzi. This dominating figure can be seen from the street, and is full of masculine energy. In the entrance hall, a series of busts of the founders leads up the main staircase. These are of four men: a statesman and antiquary, a scientist (President of the Royal Society), a politician, and a physician. They gave their own collections, of inestimable value, which became the foundation of the British Library.

The only female figure you see is quite recognizable, since she is naked—there is one naked breast peering out of the picture—and is nurturing someone who is hurt. She appears in the large tapestry 'If not, not', woven by the master weavers of the Edinburgh Tapestry Company, based on a painting by R.B. Kitaj. Amid the depiction of the horrors of war and the Holocaust, very modern imagery, the only unclothed figure, and the only nurturer, is also the only female to be included in the whole iconography of the entrance from the street to the reading rooms. The effect, once noticed, is incredibly disempowering.

Where the shape of the worshipping space, its imagery and iconography, the language and actions for worship and the experience of the worshipping community all interact, there is the potential for a truly transforming experience. The next two chapters will explore ways of enabling women's stories to encounter Scripture, and liturgy or ritual, as transformation of individual, worshipping community and the world!

Chapter Three

Using Words

During the protracted debate on the ordination of women in the Church of England, a cartoon appeared in *Punch* magazine. It showed a middle-aged, fairly 'frumpish' woman in a pulpit, evidently preaching, because she was wagging her finger at the congregation. Also in view were two members of the congregation, sitting in a pew, both middle-aged men, one of whom was saying to the other, 'I get enough of this at home'. Quite apart from what this says about the cartoonist's view of preaching, the sentiment expressed bears out the prejudice that it is all right for a man to speak authoritatively to a congregation but, when a woman does it, she is outside her sphere of authority, which is 'at home', where her authoritative speech is seen as nagging. The sense of nagging is then transferred to the woman preaching in a church.

Even more recently, ending an article in a paper to the College of Preachers, Canon Peter Kerr writes, 'In a word, many men do not like a woman telling them what to do, and so are at best ambivalent, and at worst hostile to a woman preacher and often without understanding why they are overtaken by such feelings' (Kerr 1997: 8). This is despite the report in the same article that, as preachers, men were reported as 'distant' and 'impersonal' while women were rated 'highly personal' and 'relational'.

Women's preaching is widely regarded as a new phenomenon. In this, as in other issues of women's leadership, there is a kind of spurious novelty attributable to the ordination debate in the Church of England. When I began my ministry in the late 1970s, a woman leading worship was seen as an oddity, for sure. But as the debate in the Church of England gathered momentum, the phenomenon began to be seen as 'new' by the press and the general public. This has continued since the ordination of women in the Church of England and there is a great danger that we lose touch with the longstanding tradition of women preachers in the Free Churches.

Women and Authority

It is, of course, impossible to separate *preaching*, which is the subject of this chapter, from *liturgy*, the subject of the next. Of course, the interpretation of Scripture and experience form an integral part of the liturgy. Even traditional preaching saw the Bible readings, hymns and prayers as part of a liturgical whole, whose climax came in the sermon. As the tradition of liberation and feminist hermeneutics develops, liturgy and interpretation are becoming one integrated experience. A service is a liturgical journey arising from the interaction between the worshippers, scriptural and historical narratives, and the culture or mix of cultures from which the participants come.

However, different issues arise out of women as preachers, from those which arise from women taking a sacramental role in liturgy. For sacramental traditions, the iconography of women's priesthood is at issue, and this links with theological discussions of the fullness of the image of God. In the preaching traditions, it is the authority of women's preaching that is at stake, which links with political discussions of women's role in public life as opposed to the domestic sphere. Women's authority to preach has repercussions on women's authority in the decision-making structures of churches, and their ability to challenge both religious and political bodies by prophetic utterance.

The important thing for women as preachers is that our preaching is inextricably bound up with our authority. The temptation to draw back from authoritative proclamation, in however creative a form, is always there. Marie Ropeti, writing from the perspective of the Pacific women in Aoteroa New Zealand churches, acknowledges the constant struggle with patriarchal views: 'It is much easier to survive by acquiescing to the stereotypical model and focusing on pastoral skills than by working to develop a critical philosophy of faith and theology. The temptation for women is to be domesticated rather than to be prophetic or scholarly in ways that are strong' (1995: 174).

By looking out for the hidden stories of Scripture, the reader can trace a line of women prophets and preachers. Sometimes women prophets seem to be reliable sources to be consulted in private, when circumstances are sensitive, a role that can shade over into witchcraft, if the consultant is in some kind of trouble. 1 Samuel 28.8-24, for example, tells the story of Saul's consultation with the woman of Endor. But they also had a public role.

It is clear that the prophetic bands that gathered during the period of the monarchy in Israel included women as well as men. These may well have been simply the wives of the male prophets. Isaiah calls his wife 'the prophetess' (Isa. 8.3), and their sexual act is seen as an act of prophecy in itself, since the child that is born is given the name that means 'speedy spoil, prompt plundering', and his name and childhood are linked with the destruction of the northern kingdom of Israel.

Twice, at times of critical change in the theological life of Israel, the words of prophetesses are fundamental. Just before the downfall of Jerusalem, a movement for reformation arises. The king, Josiah, instigates a refurbishment of the Temple, which has fallen into ruin and the restorers turn up (or plant) a scroll, which contains the legal and religious basis of Yahwism. It is called 'The Book of the Law'. Josiah can immediately see the significance of this, and he sends the impressively titled, entirely male group of priests and military leaders to seek advice.

The person they turn to is Huldah, a prophetess. Nowhere in the narrative is there any indication that this is strange or ironic. The reader can enjoy the perhaps anachronistic irony of the priest, the adjutant general and the king's attendant depending on a woman for advice which Josiah says is 'for the people and for all Judah'. Huldah responds with a genuine prophetic word, 'This is the word of the LORD, the God of Israel. Tell the man who sent you to me that this is what the LORD says: I am about to bring disaster on this place and its inhabitants...' (2 Kgs 22.16; see p. 83 on the use of 'LORD' for the divine name).

God has seen the disobedience of the people and intends to bring disaster upon them. Huldah is adept at interpreting the signs of the times, well versed enough in contemporary politics to understand the significance of the scroll that is before her, and confident enough in her role as a prophet to speak God's word.

Much later, when the great messianic prophecies are fulfilled in the birth of a child, it is the prophetess who proclaims the message throughout Jerusalem. When the infant Jesus was taken to be circumcised, two pious, aged Israelites recognized him as the one who was to come. Simeon sang a moving song that has become part of the Christian heritage and is sung regularly in some traditions as the Nunc Dimittis. Anna is far less well remembered, though her actions were more public. Luke

2.38 records, 'Coming up at that very moment, she gave thanks to God: and she talked about the child to all who were looking for the liberation of Jerusalem'. She may well have seeded the popular movement that greeted Jesus much later in his adult years. She was certainly the first to make his identity public.

Significantly, the first person to proclaim the resurrection of Jesus was also a woman, or women. The Gospel narratives of the resurrection are diverse in many details: who was first at the empty tomb; who exactly appeared to the first comers; what words were spoken; and so on. But they speak with one voice in giving to women the honour of being the first witnesses to the resurrection. The short ending of Mark has the women saying nothing to anyone, but various added verses tell of the women or Mary of Magdala alone carrying the news to the followers of Jesus. In Matthew's Gospel, it is Mary of Magdala and the other Mary, while Luke talks of a number of women, whose account of the resurrection at first appears to be nonsense to the apostles (Mt. 28.1-10; Lk. 24.1-11). John's Gospel tells a more complex, but very moving story. Mary of Magdala is the first to see the empty tomb and runs to tell Simon Peter and the beloved disciple. They rush to the tomb and, having seen, go home. Mary stays where she is and meets Jesus, who tells her to tell his followers.

On the other hand, the women are only entrusted with the message to the disciples or brothers of Jesus. It seems as though theirs is the domestic duty to tell the men, who then carry the message to the world. However, this is not true to the scriptural record. In Matthew's Gospel, the angel instructs the women to go and tell 'his disciples'. Later on, this is qualified as 'the eleven disciples', but elsewhere, the term refers to the followers of Jesus, male and female. Who else would the women tell, but his followers. Jesus uses the words translated, 'my brothers'. But the word 'brothers' is also the only way New Testament Greek could say, 'brothers and sisters', since the masculine plural includes the feminine. The same is true in the other accounts. The women make the first announcement of Jesus' resurrection. They tell the group of people they would most naturally go to—in Mary's words according to John, 'I have seen the Lord!'

The early church knew its women prophets and preachers, though they are played down both in the scriptural text and in translation and interpretation of the text. The greetings in Paul's letters contain the names of many women, some of whom were clearly leaders in the churches. Priscilla is perhaps the best-known woman teacher. From the number of times she and Aquila are mentioned, it is clear that their ministry is of great importance. Others are known as prophets, for example, Philip's daughters in Acts 21.9 and there are regulations for their demeanour while speaking in the congregational assembly—clearly an attempt to enforce communal power over women in their new powerful role.

Of course, one of the matters of concern to the Pauline tradition in the early church was coping with the authority of women. The epistles from this background range from inconsistency to panic on the matter, but the links between public speaking and the public role of women is quite clear. After the freedom offered to women in the nomadic life-style of the community around Jesus, the restrictions which closed in during the first years of the church must have been a shock and a disappointment—a story repeated throughout Christian history.

There are three passages that refer specifically to the role of women in worship. Some other epistles include a formula for domestic life, regulating the lives of men, women, children and slaves, but I am dealing only with those which refer specifically to worship.

The first injunction appears in 1 Cor. 11.2-16, during a discursus on the proper conduct of public worship. The whole passage deals with such subjects as the use of food consecrated to pagan idols, inequality in worship and speaking in tongues. The section on the role of women assumes that they, as well as men, will offer public leadership in prayer and prophecy. The point at issue is how the two sexes should dress: a man should have his head uncovered, while a woman should have hers covered—she 'must have the sign of her authority on her head' (v. 10, REB).

This rubric is justified by a very strange and confused jumble of reasons. Some are theological: woman is derived from man, and reflects man's glory, while man reflects God's glory. Some are social: it is shameful for women to have their heads uncovered, indeed, they may as well be shorn! And the whole sorry jumble ends with a defensive and emotional appeal: everyone agrees with me, so I must be right (v. 16)!

The important points for the purpose of this argument are that the women must dress this way while they are participating in public roles in worship alongside men, and that their head covering is a sign of authority, 'exousia'; they wear authority on their heads.

Paul's teaching on the proper conduct of worship comes to its climax through the image of the congregation as the body of Christ, with its various functions and gifts, in the glories of the greatest of gifts, love. Love is at the heart of Christian worship and Christian life. Spiritual arrogance is condemned, in the self-seeking use of glossolalia (speaking in tongues). If speakers in tongues are aware that no one is interpreting the message, they should remain silent and speak to themselves and God (14.28, REB). The aim is ecstatic but orderly worship, and the teaching comes to a close with 14.39, which follows in sense directly from 14.33.

However, the sense is interrupted by another irritable and unreasoned excursion on the role of women. Here, in direct contradiction to the earlier passage, they have no public role at all but are to keep silent. Once again, the assertion is supported by social and emotional arguments, without even the attempt at theological justification found in ch. 11. Whereas the speaker in tongues is to remain silent only while there is no interpreter, women are enjoined to silence throughout. Coming, as it does, at the close of a stretch of teaching which stresses equal participation based on the law of love, this is a shocking insertion into the epistle.

Even more repressively, the silence of women is linked to their domestic role. They are wives, and should ask their questions of their husbands at home. There is no hint of any authority here. Each woman is assumed to belong to a man. He is the public figure in the proceedings, and she participates only through him and expresses her participation only in the domestic space, never in public.

The final blow comes in the later, pastoral epistle, the first to Timothy (2.9-15). Here, dress code, silence, submission and exclusion to the domestic sphere are all undergirded by the theological argument of ontological supremacy. Women must dress modestly. They must learn gently and submissively (*hesuchia* is gentleness, quietness, not the silence enjoined on them in 1 Cor. 14). Women may not teach at all, nor have power over men. All this is based on the order of creation in Genesis 2, and sealed with the devastating conclusion that salvation, for women, is in childbearing—the condition and activity which, more than anything else, ties them to the domestic sphere.

The context of this passage is leadership in the churches. Public leadership of worship is confined to men (2.8) as is the ministry of oversight (episcopacy). While women may be deacons (sometimes translated as ministers), the norm is still male, as the deacon is to be the husband of one wife (3.12).

We are back to Elise Boulding's 'Something very remarkable nearly happened'. She writes,

> For the first hundred years of the new era, women were everywhere leaving behind old constraints, stepping into the public sphere and participating in the creation of a new society. The extent of persecution of these women by Roman authorities was a measure of the extent to which the old world feared the new roles for women. The rate at which women joined the new Christian movement was a measure of the readiness of women for the new life (1992: 340).

Despite the persistence of repression, women have found ways to authority in the practice of the Christian faith and, in doing so, have spoken and acted prophetically towards the patriarchal basis of that faith. Ruether reflects the excitement of women's authority as it resurfaces from time to time, and challenges religious, as well as social and political structures.

> Again and again throughout Christian history this antipatriarchal use of God-language has been rediscovered by dissenting groups... Throughout Christian history women discovered this concept of direct relation to God as a way to affirm their own authority and autonomy against patriarchal authority. God's call to them to preach, to teach, to form a new community where women's gifts were fully actualized overruled the patriarchal authority that told them to remain at home as dutiful daughters or wives (1985: 157).

The Church's relentless silencing of women's voices has been charted in an earlier chapter. But, throughout the life of the Church, groups have arisen which have pushed back the walls of silence and allowed women full or partial licence to preach and lead worship. In particular, the rise of modern women's preaching has its roots in the many and complex manifestations of the Reformation in the West of Europe and, later, in North America.

As the scriptures became available in English, women began to participate in teaching and interpretation in local communities in England. Women Lollards opened their homes as centres for Bible study, and began a movement of dissent, withdrawing support from the parish churches in order to support their own house churches.

In the mainstream (if there can be said to have been a mainstream) of the Reformation, women rose to positions of influence, often as the wives of Lutheran or Calvinist ministers. Barbara MacHaffie (1986: 63) writes of these, that they 'often found themselves presiding over households that were centres of cultural and intellectual activities. They offered hospitality to theologians, advice to other clergy, and bed and board to young students. Luther's wife, Catherine von Bora, presided over barnyard, fishpond, orchard, a host of servants, children, sick visitors, student boarders, and church leaders and theologians.' Katherine Zell, wife of the Strasbourg Pastor, Matthew Zell, also preached in public and spoke out against persecution in the old prophetic mode. She preached at her husband's funeral.

Outside this mainstream arose a number of independent movements, which experimented with far more radical and open democratic structures. These included Anabaptist, Quaker and other independent groups. These were often persecuted by both Catholic and Lutheran authorities. In many of these, women were allowed freedom to speak and may have been given complete equality. They challenged the patriarchal feudal systems of the secular world as well as the hierarchies of the Church.

In the Quaker movement, women and men could speak openly and freely in public worship and could witness openly in public life. Elise Boulding comments on the common reception of such witness: 'Preaching in public was one of the worst things a woman could do in the 1600s and Quaker women were continually preaching in public—in streets, in fields, wherever they could command an audience. They were in prison a great deal, often publicly whipped and always subject to having their possessions seized' (1992: 562).

The late eighteenth and early nineteenth centuries saw an awakening of spiritual experience, the revival of early dissenting denominations, and the formation of new ones. The great revivalist movements often included women evangelists and preachers. Wesley encouraged women class leaders and Bible teachers, though the ministers of congregations were all men. As the nineteenth century progressed, women found opportunities in mission work in 'the field' and evangelism 'at home'. The wives of missionaries frequently carried on the work of their husbands when they died, and single women found openings abroad which were closed to them in their own churches. In the Roman Catholic Church, some of the women's religious orders began to do pioneering work in the misson field. Boulding notes that, 'Some of the most radical developments in the contemporary Catholic Church have come from the 20th century inheritors of these sisterhood traditions' (1992: 669).

The same missionary movement in which European women found a measure of freedom and autonomy, was, of course, to a great extent, simply an arm of the imperial ambitions of European nations, which deprived many indigenous cultures of their freedom and autonomy. Sometimes the missionaries were willing collaborators in the destruction of local culture, serving to silence indigenous religious traditions as effectively as the churches silenced women's religious traditions of an earlier era in Europe. Vincent Donovan, a Roman Catholic missionary, commented that an African preacher of his acquaintance not only found it hard to use native instruments in worship, since they had been denounced as demonic, but even found it difficult to use his own language. He thought of the native language of his people as too dirty for use in Christian worship. The Christian faith brought by the missionaries totally repressed the cultural expression of the indigenous peoples. Symbolism, means of celebration and even language was overlaid by the culture of the oppressor.

Similarly shocking is the way in which feminine imagery for God, or the relation of women's experience to Christian worship, is considered 'dirty' today. Symbolism and language relating specifically to women is repressed and overlaid with male cultural expression, so that women and women's experience become invisible, or, worse, defiled.

This means that European women, at any rate, share with the missionary movement its oppressive and destructive history. But they also share with the indigenous peoples a history of oppression by the same Church. Their story as missionaries can be dismissed on the grounds that the oppressors' story will always be told. But I believe that there is room for the voice of women missionaries to be heard as part of the underside of history. Boulding suggests that, 'The encounter of women of other continents with the missionary women of Europe should properly be written as an encounter between two sets of women's cultures...It is possible that valuable information on women's activities in colonized areas can be recovered from accounts of women missionaries, who would be far more likely than men to have entered into the women's spaces' (Boulding 1992: 671).

Lavinia Byrne's book of women's writings from and about the mission field recognizes the dual nature of women as agents both of colonization and liberation. She recognizes that 'their language is racist, their preoccupation with cleanliness is unnerving...' (1991: 6). On the other hand, they frequently carried a message of liberation which challenged imperial certainties and cultural injustices alike.

What the missionary women discovered as they travelled to distant parts
of the world was that horrendous disciplines were in place which bound
women either physically, emotionally, spiritually or literally. Only a new
morality could set women free. Only a new morality could challenge
men to see things differently and to realize that the disciplines which they
had set up were so harmful to women (Byrne 1991: 6).

One section of the book shows women courageously speaking out
against the persecution of barren wives, female infanticide, child prostitution and the general pervasive devaluing of women as human beings.

Within the Holiness movement, the emphasis being on the power
and authority of the Holy Spirit, women preachers arose as a major
force. Phoebe Palmer travelled throughout the United States of America
and to Britain and Canada as an evangelist and preacher. It was through
her ministry that Catherine Booth and Frances Willard received their
calling. Frances Willard travelled with Dwight Moody and was a
preacher on social reform. She argues convincingly and in terms very
familiar to us from Scripture, that women should be allowed to preach,
as indeed, in her day, they were. She quotes from several prominent
women preachers of her day including Catherine Booth and Phoebe
Palmer as well as many less well known but established preachers and
pastors, some, of course, ordained. Men's voices are also heard, both for
and against the argument. Reading her book causes wonder that all the
arguments were known and clearly stated over 100 years ago, and
despair that they are really still so little known as to need restating constantly (Willard 1978).

Catherine Booth was, of course, partner of William Booth in inaugu-
rating the Salvation Army. History has hidden her role, but she and
William were both firmly committed to equality for women in all
spheres, including their own marriage. In the movement they founded,
many of the early preachers were young women, who took on causes in
the worst slums in London and other cities. They faced physical danger,
not only through the nature of the areas in which they worked, but also
through open hostility within the community. Women in their early 20s
quelled riots, ran Corps and preached and taught in worship and on
street corners.

Another woman influenced by Phoebe Palmer was Amanda Berry
Smith, a black washerwoman, who became an effective and prominent
Holiness preacher. Both the Church of the Nazarene and the Pilgrim
Holiness Church guaranteed the right of women to preach, the former
in its constitution of 1894.

The Holiness movement continues to offer opportunities for women to preach and prophesy. Indeed, Elizabeth Amoah draws a distinction between ordination of women in the African churches of missionary origin and in indigenous churches. In the former, 'it is difficult to avoid the suspicion that this tends to be merely decorative, as if women were ordained to satisfy some emergent trend', while in the latter, 'authority seems more centred on the Holy Spirit and charisma, and women in general are not excluded from important offices and positions. They freely perform their roles as pastors, healers and prophetesses' (Amoah 1995: 3).

In the twentieth century, the debate has tended to centre on women's ordination, but there has continued to be virulent opposition to women's right to preach in public worship. Where, however, women's voices have been heard from the pulpit, or in other forms of proclamation, this has frequently had an impact on the type of message preached and forms of preaching.

The tension between the pioneer Unitarian women ministers of the American west and the nineteenth century ministers and the Unitarian 'establishment' on the east coast is interesting in itself. But the isolation and excitement of the western churches gave rise to preaching of a radical nature, as well as the development of experimental liturgical forms.

In some senses it was the nature of their ministry which enabled ministers such as Eleanor Gordon and Mary Safford to preach a more radical message than was possible 'back east'. 'Not only was their very presence in pulpits a statement offensive to many, but their calling, most likely, had been inspired by those who had in the past been uncompromising and risked the people's wrath to preach a faith of social responsibility' (Tucker 1994: 159). They were very often contemptuous of the male preachers who either preferred the more established churches of the east, or came to the west with 'eastern' ideas. Eleanor Gordon asked the American Unitarian Association meeting, 'What is the matter with these younger ministers? They do not look for a place where they may wrestle with superstition, ignorance, materialism, godlessness, but where there is a church built, where the work has been done, where everyone is saved, where all they have to do is write an essay once a week, and perhaps lead a Browning Club' (Tucker 1994: 124).

Safford, Gordon and others took their place among the great women orators of the late nineteenth century. Mary Livermore, Julia Ward Howe, Anna Howard Shaw and others were speaking eloquently in support of social reform. So the sermons of preachers such as Caroline Bartlett Crane also tackled issues such as prostitution and prison reform.

The large and enthusiastic congregations, who flocked to hear them, were treated as participants in the argument, rather than as passive hearers. Sermons were part of the work of building up communities where justice and peace flourished. The congregation was expected to carry the message of the sermon into the practicalities of living life. Tucker writes, 'As the sisterhood saw it, successful sermons were those that made everyone "priests" and had them accept the responsibility of forming and defending their faith' (Tucker 1994: 161).

Participatory Preaching

I was brought up as a congregationalist, one of the preaching traditions, with a strong emphasis on the priesthood of all believers. I preferred as a child to listen to the sermon, rather than joining in activities provided for children. Many of the sermons I heard were scholarly and sensitive. They have helped me to form my own theology and, because of their questioning nature, raised me in a milieu in which the primary sin was failure to use the brain and the talents God gave you!

Despite the fact that women had been ordained in my own tradition long before my birth, much of the preaching I heard as a child and growing adult was by men. No doubt I absorbed a great deal of the style of preaching as well as the content. When I started lay preaching, and eventually trained as a minister, my early experience was confirmed by the kind of 'techniques' we were to use to get the message across.

Among these was the 'story'. This was used as a device to carry the point you were making, a sermon illustration. It also served a valuable purpose in recapturing the congregation's attention, which had wandered during an abstract argument, so that the preacher could go on to the next stage in the argument. In other words, the story was there to serve the sermon. The tradition was to get your theme, or your message, and then think of illustrations.

One form that the story takes in this kind of preaching is the joke. Often a sermon would begin with a joke, to get the hearers on your side. The joke is a story that is not true, and depends for its effect on shared sophistication. The congregation shows that it 'gets' the joke by laughing. The joke often sets the context by inviting laughter at the expense of the speaker. An example is the story of a little bird that was lost, flying over the Arctic wastes. The bird dropped to earth and was in danger of freezing to death. A passing hunter saw the frozen body, and took pity on it. He picked it up, cradling it in his hands and placed it in a pile of steaming dung. Sure enough, the bird warmed up and began to revive. Its feeble flutterings were spotted by an arctic fox, who pounced on the little morsel and ate it. The moral is that it is not always your enemies who land you in it, or your friends who get you out. This is used to draw down humour on to the speaker and his friends who got him into this speaking engagement. The congregation is drawn into the shared sophistication of those who 'get' the joke, and share the added frisson of what is almost a 'dirty' joke told in church.

In the style of preaching emerging as a tradition of women's preaching, stories are used in subtly different ways. Though, of course, the boundaries are blurred, in general, where men tell jokes, women create myths. This is borne out by the received wisdom that women are no good at telling jokes and therefore (by the way) make rotten after-dinner speakers. That is not to say that women's use of story-telling is devoid of humour. It uses humour in a different way.

Carol J. Schlueter, writing in *Women's Visions*, attempts to describe feminist homiletics by means of a myth which she calls the 'Canada Goose Principle'. 'Canada geese fly in a "V" formation, and no one bird is always the leader, but each takes its turn. Upon tiring, the leader drops back and another bird replaces it. The well-being of each bird is important to the survival of the flock; and the more birds that share the leadership, the easier it is for the flock to progress well (Schlueter 1995: 138). The moral of this tale, with reference to homiletics, suggests 'preparing sermons in collaboration with the ideas and experiences of others in one's context' (Schlueter 1995: 138).

This is a radical message. The model of sermon preparation under which I was trained involved setting aside a considerable amount of time 'in the study'. We thought that we were ahead of our predecessors in that we 'took the newspaper into the study' so that our preparation was carried out in the context of the daily news. But there was no sense of preparing with others. Even if worship groups were preparing the rest of the service collaboratively, the sermon was somehow sacred, and the most powerful person or person of highest status would be responsible for its preparation and delivery. There was certainly no means of the leader admitting weakness by dropping back to allow someone else to replace him or her. This formed no part of the model—the model could not be altered to include it.

At Mansfield College, Oxford, where I trained, we had a weekly sermon class. One member of the student body would take a whole service, and it would be discussed afterwards by the other students under the leadership of the principal. In the mid-1970s, the principal was George Caird, who insisted that the whole purpose of every sermon was simply to proclaim Christ crucified. The sermon was to be a logical exposition of the Christ event, related to the lives of the listeners. Even the personal attributes and life of the preacher were not to intrude in any way. Our dress and manner was to contribute to our anonymity so that the message should be unimpeded. I was even reprimanded on one occasion by opening a service with a prayer which included the words, 'We worship you'. The reprimand was that I spoke those words in a passionate way, as if by saying them, I could make them come true.

Schlueter's model of hermeneutics includes, indeed draws from, the personal experience of the preacher in the context of a group in dialogue. It is altogether closer to story-telling, though it is not non- or anti-theological. It simply sets the context of preaching in the stories of people whose voices are not generally heard. She makes the staggering assertion that, 'only the one who is involved in women's struggles should be allowed to preach' (Schlueter 1995: 139). This is right. It is not that only women should be allowed to preach, but that only those who are involved in the struggle against what hampers God's reign should dare to speak God's message. To be involved in the struggle is to listen to the voices of the abused and oppressed. 'When abused women's bodies are the hermeneutic we use to read scripture, then our sermons and lives will be passionate about social, political and ecclesial change' (Schlueter 1995: 139).

Rather than suffering, *mujerista* theology puts *la lucha*, the struggle, at the heart of self-awareness. Ada Maria Isasi-Díaz (Isasi-Díaz 1995: 91) finds this in the ability of Latin American women to celebrate. *Fiesta* is the celebration of the struggle against the powers that cause them to suffer. Rather than glorifying suffering as Christlike passivity, they engage with the injustice.

Recently, I have heard more people preaching and teaching from this kind of background. The result is not a reinterpretation of Scripture so much as corrective to the prior interpretations. Women, whose stories have not been noticed before, come to light from Scripture out of the darkness of prejudicial selective teaching. The Hebrew midwives stand up proud and strong (Exod. 1.15-21) among their people. They defied Pharaoh's edict long before Moses was heard of. Hagar, lost and alone, but chosen by God, reveals the tragedy and scandal of women abused by women of privilege (Gen. 16). The Syro-Phoenician woman's cheeky question becomes a learning point for Jesus (Mk 7.24-30), and Jesus is seen not only healing women, but setting them free from the bondage of tradition which declared them unclean.

Schlueter describes this work of rediscovery as 'Interweaving our stories with the biblical stories' (Schlueter 1995: 149). This she also unpacks as an image. The weaving will be colourful. New threads come into play while some recede. New patterns emerge from the work. There are tangles which 'keep the full pattern of women's creativity from surfacing' (Schlueter 1995: 149) as women are still silenced and only the powerful are heard. She writes, 'if the use of feminist narrative or artistic representations ignites a process of *energeia* so that we experience new visions of women as moral agents, then perhaps the tangles can be attended to lovingly and respectfully, rather than being torn out, cut off or ignored' (Schlueter 1995: 150).

Heather Walton and Susan Durber have contributed to the development of the tradition of women's preaching by producing a book of women's sermons (1994). The book reveals a great variety in women's preaching, which is only to be expected. The compilers reflect on the variety and draw out various principles which seem to arise from the tradition.

Quite clearly from the collection emerges a powerful emphasis on the experience of women. The writers draw on their own, often harrowing experiences: sexual abuse; the death of a baby; a hysterectomy; failure to conceive. These are experiences of a kind which generally remain completely unspoken in church. By setting personal experience alongside biblical narrative, the Bible, its characters and stories, speak in new and quite startling ways.

Mary Cotes's tremendously powerful description of the birth of Jesus describes the compelling pain and rhythm of the birthing process, and the messiness of the circumstances into which Jesus is born. She uses this to puncture the complacency of the Christmas carols with their picture of perfection and, above all, silence. She says, 'We have wanted women whose pain need never come to our ears and children whose crying need not be heard' (Cotes 1994: 7). Instead, the God of the incarnation outrages the delicacy which regards bodily functions such as birth-giving as unspeakable and breaks through the complacency which permits Christmas worship to take place in hallowed surroundings far from the anguish of the world.

Heather Walton exposes her own infertility in a thought-provoking critique of class and culture distinction. She faces squarely her own privileged life and background, comparing herself with Pharaoh's daughter in the story of Moses. The Hebrew women are fertile. Pharaoh's daughter has wealth and power. The people of Israel exist under oppression. Out of this set of events comes liberation, not because Pharaoh's daughter uses her power directly, nor by means of her transferring her privileged lifestyle to the child and cutting him off from his own culture.

She concludes, 'Pharaoh's daughter had brought to the centre of power a force that will destroy its dominion... It is a terrible thing to help to pull down the pillars of your own palace but sometimes God does not give us the role of bringing life but sharing in the destruction of what must die' (Walton 1994: 76).

This style of preaching interweaves the Bible narratives as real stories with the real stories of women's and men's lives. The direction of the flow of logic is no longer all one way. Traditional preaching uses Scripture to define and prescribe the ways of human life. Because the Bible says this, this is the way you should live; this is the way you should feel. As the Bible is used in a prescriptive way, experience which does not conform is denied or hidden.

Perhaps the most dramatic example of this is when someone's life-experience makes it difficult or impossible to receive what the Bible insists is God's gifts of healing, forgiveness, new life and unconditional love. At its worst, the argument is reversed, to insist that anyone who does not find healing, does not live a perfectly blessed Christian life, basking in God's wonderful love, and must not be a Christian. Justification by faith is supposed to remove the burden of achieving salvation from the individual. God's forgiving and healing love is simply there to be received. The trouble is that faith itself is so damned strenuous!

The style of preaching revealed in this collection allows the experience of women to interact with scriptural record. 'Carol' writes from the experience of sexual abuse. Her experience has two profound effects on the way she receives traditional teaching. First, talk of love and forgiveness may actually mean nothing to one who has never known them. 'Telling a person who has never felt unconditional love that this is what God's love is like is meaningless. Telling a person whose smallest childhood misdemeanours were rarely forgiven and even more rarely forgotten that God forgives people's sins and "wipes them out" is just a form of words' ('Carol' 1994: 58).

But as a survivor of sexual abuse, 'Carol' is aware of the contribution of her own story. The logic of scripture does not flow all one way, from the Bible to the life of the woman. She says, 'I have experiences to offer. I have *my* expereinces to offer—*my* story, *my* song. The Exodus, the Exile, the Valley of the Shadow and the Passion. All these—and true resurrection' ('Carol' 1994: 59).

So women preach from their own experience and, as a tradition of women's preaching develops, this becomes more marked. Women become more and more free from the necessity to ape male forms of preaching or stick to traditions not their own. This in itself leads to new and powerful ways of using scriptural sources. It is not only that experience and Scripture interact far more openly and honestly than was the norm. Stories and voices from Scripture are being heard which have long been ignored.

Traditional preaching focuses on the majesty and power of God, and the normality of a happy, prosperous life for God's people. Suffering is confined to Jesus, and to the way of life that is passing away. Christians are enjoined to enter into God's happiness, to find in Scripture stories, rules and maxims which hallow the cosiness of their own lives and which support the norms of their own culture. Where those norms are used to oppress and cause suffering, the very Christlikeness of suffering is used to reinforce oppression. Sufferers are hallowed with a veneer of martyrdom, which may even create a sado-masochistic structure, in which the oppressed are supposed to enjoy their status as victims.

What is happening not only in feminist preaching, but also in liberation preaching of all kinds, is that the uncomfortable, discordant, challenging voices of Scripture are heard again. Women, like other groups marginalized from power, speak from the chaotic edges of the world known to powerful men. Therefore their words and their stories, their use of Scripture tend to overturn the norms and disrupt cosy lives.

As has been said, marginalization is complex; sometimes women are found speaking for the oppressor and sometimes men are found among the oppressed. Nevertheless, female gender is a reason for marginalization on its own, and women share the experience of being excluded simply on the basis on their sex as well as being involved variously in other structures of oppression. In fact, Heather Walton's sermon, quoted above, reflects on the awareness of being an oppressor as well as being under oppression.

So long as we retain this kind of awareness, the risk of telling our stories is in itself a subversive act. It challenges a style of preaching that uses stories only as illustrations; it troubles the steady stream of prescription from Scripture by introducing cross-currents, rapids and backwaters of experience; and it uncovers a reality which traditional preaching has too often pretended did not exist or could be 'cured'. Carol Christ takes the argument one step further back when she writes, 'Women have lived in the interstices between inchoate experiences and the shapings given to experience by the stories of men. In a very real sense, women have not experienced their own experience' (1992a: 228). She goes on, 'Telling our stories may possibly begin a great revolution, unleashing the power to turn the world's great order round' (1992a: 243).

Women are appalled by the complacency of traditional preaching. Margaret Kennedy cries out on behalf of survivors of sexual abuse, 'There is no condemnation from the pulpits, no liturgies of support and compassion, no prayer or sermons… How is it we so quickly ask survivors to forgive and forget and never ask for justice for the survivor' (1994: 16-17). Jenny Spouge reports the cry of people who have faced loss of employment, 'Why do we not hear such alternative value systems preached from the pulpit?' and says that, 'As a preacher, I stand condemned by that cry' (1994: 2). While women preachers, of whom there are many, reject the imperative to speak from their own experience of marginalization, while we continue in a style of preaching which bolsters up the complacency of the powerful, God's justice continues to be unheard.

This is far more important than an argument about preaching styles. It is a question of whether the true and valid call of God will be heard or silenced. A feminist homiletic challenges the interpretation of Scripture. But the emerging tradition of women's preaching has developed new and exciting means for the worshipping community sharing in the story and its interpretation.

At its simplest, the 'sermon' may take the form of a dialogue between a preacher and a congregation. This happens in several contexts. At a recent baptism service in my own church, several children from one family were baptized. They ranged from the white of the father to the black of the mother. After the service, a woman from the mother's family expressed her frustration at having to stay silent during the service, and particularly during the sermon. She was used to a lively interchange between the preacher and the congregation, building up to an enthusiastic climax to which the preacher and the congregation contributed.

Listening in respectful silence is actually the experience of only a few Christian traditions. As it serves to silence all but the speaker, it adds to the silencing of women. In more participative cultures, women's voices are freed to be heard not only in the pulpit but in the responding congregation. Ofelia Ortega edited a compilation of different cultural expression in *Women's Visions* (1995). Preaching patterns include discussion, the use of visual material, drama and participation in spontaneous story-telling.

Elizabeth Amoah comments, 'African women who are not formally educated express their theology in the spontaneous, poetic lyrics, songs and prayers which are an ordinary part of their everyday lives. In the African instituted churches women freely involve themselves in preaching, prophesying, healing and counselling' (Amoah 1995: 1). Sun Ai-Lee Park describes the process of the Ecumenical Association of Third World Theologians commission on women, whose insights were developed in the story-telling ministries of Korea (Lee-Park 1995: 44). The emerging tradition of women theologians and preachers working together in Latin America gives rise to 'Great creativity...in presentation: besides analytical biblical studies we find meditations and poetic reflections of great biblical-theological depth, symbolically rich combinations of liturgy and biblical reflection and excellent Biblio-dramas in which the whole community can assume the role of biblical personalities, bringing in their own current concerns' (Tamez 1995: 87).

It is, then, fundamentally important that liturgy and preaching open up means of intepreting the scriptures from the point of view of women's experience, and that this is done in new and creative ways. The flow of meaning *from* Bible *to* experience in traditional worship must be challenged, so that scripture and experience develop meaning through dialogue. However, the danger of unthinkingly following this pattern is that biblical scholarship, which deals directly with the text, is devalued and patriarchal readings and interpretations are themselves left unchallenged.

Worshippers Challenging Traditions

For the biblical text itself has been read, translated and transmitted over the centuries in ways which reinforce its patriarchal nature, or introduce a male bias where it does not exist in the original. It is important that this is recognized, so that feminist liturgy and preaching is engaging with the best possible scholarship of Scripture. Otherwise we may end up tilting at windmills.

In the New Testament, for example, there is a list of greetings in Romans 16. This is an unusually long list, in which there is a high proportion of women. However, variant readings actually reduce the number of women and prejudicial translation limits their role. Verse 7 refers to Junia, who is described as related to Paul, and eminent among the apostles. Most early versions read 'Junias', a male name. Young's analytical concordance even states that this 'ought to be Junias' (1975: 559), presumably on the basis that a woman could not be included among the apostles and greeted with such respect by Paul.

Phoebe is the very first name in the list. She is called a *diakonos* (the ending is masculine, since there is no feminine ending for a compound noun in Greek). The Authorized Version translates this word as 'minister' everywhere but here, where it is translated as 'servant'. So Paul is called a 'minister of the Lord' (Col. 1.23), but Phoebe is a 'servant'. Matthew Black's commentary on Romans says, 'This seems to be the only NT reference to a deaconess. It has been conjectured that Phoebe's duties were concerned especially with women, the sick or "aliens", or with assisting women at baptism, but there is very little foundation for these speculations' (Black 1973: 178-79).

On such flimsy foundations, constructed of mistranslation and speculation, is built the whole edifice of a separate diaconate for women, devoid of authority and focused on work with particular groups in society. It is extraordinary. The Revised English Bible, on the other hand, translates accurately, 'Phoebe, a fellow-Christian, who is a minister in the church at Cenchreae' (Rom. 16.1).

In modern translations, as well as divisions into chapters and verses (which are themselves far later than the texts) there are often divisions between sections, with headings. This can also be used to shift emphasis. For example, in Ephesians 5, if an editor is going to introduce a new section between instructions to individuals about Christian living, which begin in ch. 4, and instructions about relationships, which go on to 6.9, it is fundamentally important where the line is drawn.

The New International Version of Scripture which supports an evangelical theology, inserts a new heading between vv. 21 and 22 of ch. 5. Therefore the instructions on conduct end with the sentence, 'Submit to one another out of reverence for Christ', and the new section begins with the words, 'Wives, submit to your husbands as to the Lord'. The link between general subjection to one another and the subjection of wives is broken, and the new section begins with the injunction to wives.

The Revised English Bible inserts the new heading between vv. 20 and 21, so that the section on Christian conduct ends, '…in the name of our Lord Jesus Christ give thanks every day for everything to our God and Father'. The new section begins, 'Be subject to one another out of reverence for Christ. Wives be subject to your husbands…' As people choosing Bible readings are likely to be influenced by the general divisions suggested by the translation they are using—it would be very difficult, for example, to start a reading with the last verse of the previous section—editorial decisions about lay-out have theological significance and are certainly made on that basis.

The Hebrew scriptures present a different set of problems. One arises from the convention of the Massoretic editors of Scripture[1] to replace the consonants of the divine name, which was at that time considered too holy to speak, with the vowels of a euphemism. Hebrew is written in consonants, with the vowels appearing as dots and symbols around the consonants, known as 'pointing'. It is quite possible for Hebrew to be 'unpointed', that is, to be printed without vowels. Modern Israeli newspapers are printed in this way. Therefore, it is also possible to substitute the pointing of one word for that of another, which gives rise to an actually unreadable word.

The divine name, unpointed, appears as a tetragrammaton (four letters) 'YHWH'. The convention was to indicate that the word whose vowels, or pointing, appeared was the word that should be read. In the case of the divine name, the pointing indicated that the word *'adonai'* or 'Lord' should be read instead of the divine name. The word 'Jehovah', by the way, is the result of trying to read the consonants of the divine name with the vowels of *'adonai'* and is really a non-word. English

---

1.   The Massoretic text was the work of two groups of scholars, known as the Massoretes, from the sixth to the tenth centuries CE. It is a detailed scholarly work, and set out to produce the final version of the Hebrew text.

translations have tried to accommodate the sensitivities of Hebrew by using the word 'Lord', but to show that it is not the actual word used, they have put it in capital letters 'LORD'.

In fact, rather than showing that a word has been substituted, this gives enormous emphasis to the word that is used. For example, Ps. 29.3-5 in the Revised English Bible reads, 'The voice of the LORD echoes over the waters; the God of glory thunders; the LORD thunders over the mighty waters, the voice of the LORD in power, the voice of the LORD in majesty. The voice of the LORD breaks the cedar trees, the LORD shatters the cedars of Lebanon.' This intensely triumphalistic psalm is made even more violent by the capitalized 'LORD'. It would be difficult, in reading it aloud, not to place extra emphasis on the word because of the capitalization. A glance through the Psalms will show how prevalent the use of this convention is.

Indeed, the emphasized word 'Lord' has come into the liturgical language of the Christian churches; in particular, in churches of an evangelical theology, which focus on a strong male God. It is often used with great fervour in extempore prayer and in preaching. The fact that it is not the word used in Scripture, but merely a convention, is deemed irrelevant, or is unknown.

Attempts have been made to find another convention. Sylvia Rothschild, writing in *An A to Z of Feminist Theology*, comments, 'the tetragrammaton is above issues of gender or of imagery. Translated as "The Eternal One", "Being", "The One Who Is", "The Omnipresent", "You", or even "Source of Life", it transcends the sexual politics inherent in many of the other names of God, which by describing particular attributes become available to gender manipulation' (1995: 245).

The Jerusalem Bible and New Jerusalem Bible use the divine name itself, but this may be offensive to Jewish participants in an act of worship. In any case, feminist liturgists should be aware of the issue, and choose their version of Scripture with care.

Words for the Spirit of God are variously feminine and neuter in Hebrew and Greek. The convention of calling the Holy Spirit 'he' (particularly, again, in evangelical circles) arises from the only passage of Scripture which deals with the Spirit at any great length: the farewell discourses of Jesus in John 13–17. In these, John, as often, twists the language to make his point. Although the word *pneuma* is neuter, he uses the masculine pronoun. This is incorrect Greek, but John is at liberty to make poetic use of the language. The point is that it is John's

Greek, not Jesus' Aramaic which is twisted. We have no evidence that Jesus used masculine pronouns instead of the feminine ones which would have been appropriate to his language. The purpose, presumably to make the Spirit of God personal rather than an object (it), also makes an originally female term for God male.

There is a strong argument for translating the pronouns used of the Spirit of God in the Hebrew Scriptures by female pronouns. Indeed, there is no reason not to. The decision, however, is neatly avoided, since there are very few occasions, if any, when it is appropriate to use any pronouns for the Spirit. The figure appears rarely, and never at any length. Therefore, although the female forms of verbs are used in Hebrew, there is never very much 'grammar' around to make the point come over in translation.

The same kind of thing happens in John's Gospel in the prologue, where the 'Word', 'Logos', is grammatically masculine. Translators have a dilemma. Do they translate the pronouns as 'it', as you would in any other use of the word, 'Word', or do they use the masculine form, 'he'? In general, modern translations have followed the Authorized Version in translating with the masculine pronoun. The decision, unavoidable in translation into English, has serious implications for interpretation of the second person of the Trinity.

This passage is well worth examining, since it is used in the very popular liturgies at Christmas time. The decision about pronouns is important, since it is hard to get away without at least four pronouns in quick succession: the Revised English Bible has 'He was with God at the beginning, and through him all things came to be; without him no created thing came into being. In him was life...' The reinforced masculinity is all in the English.

Where the passage turns to the identity of those who accept the Word, the situation is worse. The Authorized Version translates that God gives to them, 'power to become the sons of God...born, not of blood, nor of the will of the flesh nor of the will of man, but of God'. The sonship of believers is based on the only-begotten-sonship of the Word. But a whole descriptive phrase has been mistranslated. Traditional translations suggest a break between birth by man's sinful desire and birth as a son of God. This is seen as breaking the chain of original sin which entails that birth follows the essentially sinful act of sexual intercourse.

Certainly, the contrast is between human and divine birth, but human birth is desribed in far more down-to-earth terms. The child of God is born 'not of blood, nor of male desire, but of God'. Both female and male participation in the birth of a child of God is denied. This is not the conquest of original sin, linked inextricably to sexual lust, but the beginning of a new kind of life, which does not depend on physical conception and birth.

The patriarchal slant of translation and interpretation of Scripture is yet further exacerbated by the setting in which most people encounter Scripture and by the selection of passages presented.

Bible Society statistics show that 38% of regular churchgoers seldom or never read the Bible (Bible Society 1998). This suggests that few people, even among those who are regular attenders at church services, are reading the Bible at home or encountering biblical material in any other context than as passages read out in church. This means that the selection of passages for reading at Sunday services actually represents the sum total of Scripture that many people will hear or read. In most lectionaries, that selection reinforces the patriarchal message of church life and cuts worshippers off from the challenge of marginalized stories or prophecies. The lectionary, or the selection made by the worship leader, is, therefore, an enormously powerful tool for manipulating popular understanding of God.

Schüssler Fiorenza (1985) identifies three ways in which the power of the lectionary is exercised over the content of worship: by giving undue importance to passages selected for Sundays, over those used on other days; by treating certain passages selectively, so that some material is seen as the core, and other verses are marginalized; by using the conjunction of readings so that they form an interpretative whole.

In general, passages selected for reading focus on male characters to the exclusion of female characters, thus increasing the already disproportionate emphasis given to males in Scripture. By careful attention to the number of verses included, or by suggesting that verses may be omitted from longer readings, this disproportion is increased still further. Regina A. Boisclair notes that lectionaries used in the Roman Catholic Church 'tend to omit passages that introduce women, eliminate women from approved shorter readings, hide women in long lections and emphasize passages that reinforce patriarchal presupposition' (1994: 113).

Stories about women in the Hebrew scriptures are all but ignored, except where women appear as characters in stories about men. Thus Sarah appears as an adjunct to the story of Abraham, but Hagar's struggle with Sarah is omitted. Stories of David's rise to power are well known, and David and Jonathan become a model of firm friendship. But David's treatment of Michal is never mentioned, nor are the miseries that existed within his family as his arrogation of power became a role model for his sons.

In the Gospels, selections suggest that the active followers of Jesus were male. Accounts that show women in submissive roles are included, for example, the woman who washed Jesus' feet. But the Markan account of the woman who anointed his head—a priestly and royal action—is omitted, despite its prominent position immediately before the last supper, and despite the saying of Jesus, prefiguring the last supper, that the story would be told 'in memory of her' wherever the gospel was proclaimed (Mk 14.9). Similarly, the words and actions of the women at the tomb may be omitted from the long resurrection readings, if desired.

Occasionally, Jesus images God as a woman. These passages are also often excised from accounts to be read. The parables of the kingdom in Matthew 13 may not include the woman kneading dough, and the stories of God's love in Luke 15 are often edited to include the lost sheep and the prodigal son, but not the woman and the lost coin, which lies between them.

The Acts and epistles are used in such a way as to select out the exciting and substantial contribution made by women to the early church. Boisclair notes, 'Early Christian women are all but eliminated from the lectionary and the witness they could provide to contemporary congregations is unremembered and uncelebrated' (1994: 118-19). However, passages regulating the behaviour of women in church and society are included, again with highly manipulative selectivity. Schüssler Fiorenza points out the way in which Eph. 5.21-23 is used to include teaching about wives' submission to husbands, but stop short of advice about fathers and children and masters and slaves which form an integral part of the original passage. This, she says, implies 'that the text advising subjection of wives to husbands and identifying the husband with Christ is still valid in a way that the similar advice to other groups—children, slaves—is not' (Schüssler Fiorenza 1985: 58).

Schüssler Fiorenza's work is based on the North American Common Lectionary. In the 1990s, churches in Britain that used lectionaries agreed to follow *The Revised Common Lectionary* of 1992, based on an earlier *Common Lectionary* of 1983. In some of the above examples from the New Testament, the situation is improved. The story of the woman who anointed Jesus' head is included in the longer reading for Palm/Passion Sunday (which is very long, being over a chapter), but omitted from the shorter reading, which, at 39 verses, is more likely to be read.

On the other hand, the parable of the lost coin is included, and the three parables of God's love in Luke 15 are spread over two weeks; the woman kneading dough is read at the beginning of a reading which includes the other shorter parables of the kingdom. And Eph. 5.21–6.9 is not read.

In the Hebrew scriptures, the picture is not so good. The song of Moses is included (Exod. 15), but not the song of Deborah (Judg. 5), though part of the prose version of her story is told, from Judges 4. Hannah's song is appointed to be read in full. The female figure of Wisdom is well represented. Proverbs 8.22-31 is appointed to be read on Trinity Sunday, with Psalm 8, whose image of God is altogether more masculine and Prov. 9.1-6, the 'holy brothel', also included.

Hagar's story is still omitted. Of David's encounters, the seduction of Bathsheba and murder of Uriah is told; but neither the friendship between David and Jonathan nor his on-off marriage with Michal appears.

Some female images of God are included: for example, Isa. 66.10-14, in which the returned exiles are suckled by Jerusalem and comforted by mother God, 'As a mother comforts her son, so shall I myself comfort you' (v. 13); and Hosea 11, where God laments that the son who has been fed and taught to walk by God is now rebellious.

Lectionaries are supported by a wealth of dependent liturgical material and so have an influence on the worshipping life of God's people beyond the simple selection of Scripture passages for reading. As more traditions come together in agreement on the use of lectionaries, there is increasing pressure on other material to follow the same pattern. For example, the *Prayer Handbook*, published by the United Reformed Church but edited by an individual working with a committee drawn from some of the independent and presbyterian traditions in England, Scotland and Wales, has moved inexorably towards the lectionary.

As a member of that committee and a member of a tradition that does not, in general, make use of lectionaries, I argued against this. As editor for three years, I produced, I imagine, the last prayer book in the series ever to have been based on the editors and writers' selection of Scripture passages. I received letters of protest from users in churches who found the link to some lectionary essential so that the book could be used in weekly worship. In my third year, the link with the joint four-year lectionary was reinforced by beginning the year in Advent and not at the beginning of the calendar year. There is nothing wrong with this, but it illustrates a kind of general conforming pressure.

Books of worship material are coming out, based on the new common lectionary. Hymnbooks include selections of hymns based on lectionary passages. Writing for the lectionary is at present a way of getting published.

But the effect is even more widespread and longterm than this. The insidious manipulation of Bible knowledge through the selection of stories heard in public worship has had a huge influence on the whole of worship and writing for worship. Recently, a woman writer submitted a hymn for inclusion in *Worship Live*. It was a hymn of confidence in God, with the chorus, ' "Whatever I do, you can do", God said', and drew on the examples of Abraham, Moses, Samuel, David and Paul. When I questioned the entirely male examples of courage and confidence in God, and suggested a few women who might serve, the writer's response was saddening. She said that, in a short song, instant recognition of the characters was important, and that the women of Scripture were not sufficiently well known to be included. She added that the character she herself identified with most in Scripture was Peter.

While writers of hymns and other liturgical material base their work on stories made known by lectionary or other selections from Scripture for public worship, women's stories are doomed to remain hidden and the women of Scripture unsung.

Where providers of catechetical, Bible study or children's material also base their weekly sessions on the lectionary, the process is complete. The advantage is that children and adults in a church will be following a common set of themes through the year. The pay-off is that the silence of women begins in the child's first encounter with church. Girls find no stories about their experience, and learn that active participants in God's story are men and sometimes boys, but never girls or women except as adjuncts to the stories of men, or passive recipients of action by others. Above all, they learn that God is always, only and uncompromisingly male.

However, this is not to argue that somehow selecting passages from Scripture for worship can be avoided. It is to argue for awareness of the power of that process and alertness to what is being omitted, whether in the use of a lectionary or in the selection made by whoever leads worship in a congregation. It also argues for wider exposure to Scripture than most Christians currently have. There are sections of Scripture which may well not be suitable for public worship, but which serve as a corrective to the patriarchal texts. For example, it is important that the story of Tamar is told (2 Sam. 13) as part of the overall story of David and the rise of monarchy in Israel. But such a gruelling account could only be included, in a general act of worship, with the greatest sensitivity.

Such wider exposure is accessible to Christians who are open to it, through the study of feminist theology at various levels, through Bible studies and discussion material for congregations, through alternative and specialized acts of worship, for example, rituals for survivors of abuse, and by the introduction of feminist or inclusive lectionaries.

Schüssler Fiorenza proposes a set of principles which would govern the selection made in a feminist lectionary, given that the traditional lectionary's 'hermeneutical principles fail to take women seriously as active, significant agents in salvation history' (1985: 59). A feminist lectionary, then, springs from a feminist hermeneutic, which is wider than the simple inclusion of women's stories. It must release the strong current of scriptural writing which opposes the misuse of power and supports the empowerment of the humble and meek.

Therefore, Schüssler Fiorenza argues, a feminist lectionary could not include any texts requiring submission to power. On the one hand, not only Eph. 5.21-23 would be omitted, but the whole of the passage to 6.9, as well as, for example, Rom. 13.1-6, which commends submission to the state. On the other hand, passages that proclaim resurrection victory over death would be included. She writes that such texts, if they genuinely transcend their patriarchal origins, need not mention women at all in order to be emancipating' (Schüssler Fiorenza 1985: 60), and she includes under this heading, Rom. 8.31-39, Gal. 5.1 and Eph. 6.10-20. This last would be excluded by others on the grounds that military imagery is to be avoided.

Certainly, a feminist lectionary must bring narratives and imagery of women back into liturgical use. This includes accounts of God working through women, which should be recalled and celebrated. There are lively, humorous, moving stories of strong women participating in the work of God, and Miriam, Sarah, Deborah, the various Marys, the unnamed women who encountered Jesus, Priscilla and Phoebe all deserve to be back in the picture.

But Schüssler Fiorenza would also include accounts of the suffering and struggle of women, the 'texts of terror' of Phyllis Trible (Trible 1992b), on the grounds that these represent the experience of women today. She also directly identifies the suffering of women with the suffering figure of Jesus as a victim of violence and abuse at the centre of the Christian faith. She writes, 'To identify the suffering of women with the sufferings of Christ is not to subsume or legitimate the sufferings of women but to recognise that the abuse is blasphemy and an offence against God' (Schüssler Fiorenza 1985: 61).

If this is done, it is essential that the stories are interpreted from the point of view of women who are suffering, and not from the point of view of society which wishes to sentimentalize and condone the suffering of those whom it wishes to marginalize. For generations, the Christian faith has used Scripture to glorify suffering, seeing Jesus as the model of the perfect, uncomplaining victim, to be taken as a role-model by all those who are victimized, thus absolving the abuser of responsibility for their pain. Any concept of justice in the present age has been excluded, and the desire for it denounced as selfishness and unChristlike behaviour.

When texts are interpreted from the perspective of suffering people, there is always a call for justice. An example can be given in the interpretation of the Beatitudes by Dyanchand Carr, an Indian liberation theologian (1990). For generations, these have been used to extol meekness, gentleness, poverty of spirit, and a mournful, defeated attitude to life. They are therefore used as a tool of the oppressor, confirming the oppressed in their defeat by calling their state 'blessed'.

Paradoxically, the blessing itself is emptied of content, otherwise the radical nature of the Beatitudes would be unavoidable. The sense stops at, for example, 'blessed are the meek', and does not go on to 'for they shall inherit the earth'. William Barclay, whose extended commentaries formed the preaching of a generation of ministers and lay preachers, devotes three pages of commentary to the interpretation of the word, 'meek'. At the very end, he simply repeats the phrase, 'inherit the earth', without interpretation. His expanded form of the Beatitude reads, 'O the bliss of the man who is always angry at the right time and never angry at the wrong time, who has every instinct, and impulse, and passion under control because he himself is God-controlled, who has the humility to realise his own ignorance and his own weakness, for such a man is a king among men!' (Barclay 1956: 93).

Carr's interpretation from a liberation perspective links the Beatitudes with the manifesto of Isaiah 61. Jesus used this passage very specifically in Luke 4, and it may well have shaped this more reflective teaching. The poor, the meek and the mourners all appear in Isaiah 61 as recipients of God's favour. The Isaiah passage refers directly to his hopes for the new community following the return from exile. The blessings are substantial, a place in the restoration of Jerusalem, interpreted by Jesus as possession of God's reign, consolation for sorrow and inheritance of the earth. Inheritance itself is a powerful concept. In the first entry into the land it described each family's and tribe's inalienable title to the land. In this light, Mt. 5.3-5 describes not a blessing on poverty and mourning, but a message of release and hope, with tangible and real blessings.

The rest of the Beatitudes, according to Carr, are directed at others who are not among the poor, but can demonstrate solidarity with them. They are blessed when they hunger and thirst for *dikaiosyne*, which can be translated as 'righteousness', in which case the blessing refers to private morality and anchors the whole set of Beatitudes in personal and private life. But an equally good translation is 'justice', which places the teaching firmly in the area of social change. Their solidarity shows itself in mercy, purity and peace-making, and their blessing is to find their place alongside the poor in God's new community of justice.

Naming the Demons

Where texts have been used to perpetuate masochism on the part of women who suffer, by glorifying suffering and denouncing the longing for justice, there is real anger to be expressed. There is a need to recognize and express the hurt and harm that has been done in the name of the Church by the misuse of Scripture in worship. There is a requirement for repentance, not on the part of the victims of this misuse, but on the part of the perpetrators.

Sally Ann McReynolds and Ann O'Hara Graff talk about naming sin: 'To open the theological conversation about sin through the lens of women's experience is both to explore uncharted territory and to begin the work of exorcism, naming the demons that have worked their (often hidden) evil on us' (McReynolds and O'Hara Graff 1995: 161). Exorcism is a ritual act of naming and casting out demons. It is a powerful ceremony, since the demonic force of what is cast out is momentarily on the loose in the company, and strong emotions can be released.

Rosemary Radford Ruether describes an exorcism of patriarchal texts, in which a bell, candle and Bible are assembled as for any traditional exorcism, but the object to be exorcised is the Bible itself. Various texts are read out: Ruether's suggestions include Lev. 12.1-5 (uncleanliness of women after childbirth), Eph. 5.21-23 (male headship over women compared to the relation between Christ and the Church) and 1 Pet. 2.18-20 (slaves exhorted to accept unjust suffering from their masters as a way of sharing in Christ's crucifixion). At the end of each reading, the bell is rung, the book is held up and the community cries out in unison, 'Out, demons, out!' At the end of the ceremony, one participant says, 'These texts and all oppressive texts have lost their power over our lives. We no longer need to apologize for them or try to interpret them as words of truth, but we cast out their oppressive message as expressions of evil and justifications of evil' (Ruether 1985: 137).

A similar ritual among Korean feminist liturgists is described by Mary T. Rattigan (1995: 164-65). This is a shamanistic exorcism of *han*, which is a kind of embodiment of the acute pain of communal suffering. The first step in the ritual is breaking the silence and telling the story publicly—the community must hear the story. Secondly, the source of the suffering is named. The third step is to change the unjust situation by action. *Han-pu-ri* involves dancing, singing and weeping as a means of dealing with the pain.

A characteristic of this ritual is that it can deal with the suffering of 'ghosts'—the dead who have suffered. Rattigan quotes one particular example in relation to the 'comfort women' who were treated as commodities, brutally abused, suffered and often died at the hands of the Japanese soldiers. At the moment, the story is being told and the global community is beginning to hear. The source of suffering has been named, but there is as yet no commitment to changing the situation by acknowledging the depth of the injustice.

In Ruether's *Women-Church*, the exorcism of the Bible is followed by a 'Litany of Disaffiliation from Patriarchal Theology' (1985: 137-40), in which misogynistic texts from the patriarchal theologians are read. The exorcism was performed at a St Hilda Community meeting, with dramatic results:

> After hearing read aloud all the Bible passages which denigrate women, the anger and depression felt by the women present was so strong that one woman found it extremely difficult to receive or give absolution to the men seated on either side of her. We stopped the liturgy for a discussion and venting of feelings (Fageol 1991: 21).

The move from naming the evil, through anger and repentance to forgiveness and absolution, could not be completed within the one ritual time. When real hurts are exposed, it may not be possible to move from anger to forgiveness for a long time, or, perhaps, ever completely. Around the time of the millennium, people are beginning to understand that Jesus' mandate to forgive is not facile, and that the onus is on the perpetrator of the wrong to engage in true and full repentance, rather than on the victim to offer freedom from responsibility through forgiveness.

This has long been recognized in communities such as survivors of abuse. An act of worship which Christian Survivors of Sexual Abuse permitted me to publish has caused very mixed reactions among discussion groups to which I have taken it. At one point in the service, after the telling of stories and much weeping, the participants went out into the garden to let off fireworks. As the fireworks shot into the sky, the participants cried out in anger against their abusers: 'There goes my *brother*!' Margaret Kennedy says, 'Lighting the fireworks was hilarious, fun, serious, painful, freeing, wonderful, all sorts of emotions. They whistled and banged in the air.' She describes one survivor waving a sparkler with an expression that seemed to say, 'I am a survivor—I am proud—I am wonderful—I did nothing wrong' (Kennedy 1995: 3).

Many people, in discussion groups, find this account extremely moving. Others, generally traditional Christians, are deeply troubled because it talks of anger and justice, but not forgiveness. Shouldn't they be trying to forgive their abusers?

With Christian Survivors of Sexual Abuse, I have looked at the teaching of Jesus on forgiveness. Customarily, we begin with the conversation between Jesus and Peter, in which Jesus says that we must be ready to forgive, not seven times, but seventy times seven times (Mt. 18.21-22). This teaching is followed by a parable which indicates that nothing we have suffered and need to forgive can stand comparison with what God has suffered from us and is ready to forgive (vv. 23-35). This is the classic martyrdom message and it is found as a whole reading (vv. 21-35) in the Revised Common Lectionary.

But if the passage is set in context, the message about unconditional forgiveness is by no means so clear. The preceding verses (15-16) describe the process of dealing with an offender. Forgiveness is not the first option, nor is it necessarily the final outcome. The first action is to confront the sinner with the sin. If a personal approach does not work, then the matter must be discussed by a small group, so that the accusation can be seen to be fair. If the situation is still not resolved, the matter is taken up by the whole community, which has the power to declare the sinner unforgiven. This power not to forgive is repeated in Jn 20.23.

Going further back into the passage, the consequences of sin on the sinner and the community are clearly set out. This is no facile requirement to let bygones be bygones: 'if anyone causes the downfall of one of these little ones who believe in me, it would be better for him to have a millstone hung round his neck and be drowned in the depths of the sea' (Mt. 18.6). In the Hebrew scriptures, of course, the sea, or the deep, is a symbol of hell, the godless chaos which threatens to break in on God's order and rob people of their hope and their lives (e.g. Ps. 69.1-2; 130.1). This is not just a brutal punishment, it is the symbolic equivalent to being cast into outer darkness.

The appropriate reaction in the face of violence or abuse is anger, the raging desire that the perpetrator may be punished. Only then comes a strategy for bringing the perpetrator back into the community, and even then, this is only possible if he or she recognizes the wrong and repents. It may not be possible at all. The anger felt by the woman after the ritual to exorcise patriarchal and oppressive passages from Scripture was fully justifiable in Scripture's own terms. The demonic power of patriarchy was exposed and community was no longer possible. She could not express or receive forgiveness at that point. Holy anger is the appropriate reaction, and may be the final reaction.

The same issues arise in respect of repentance liturgies which try to address some of the huge injustices of the last century and millennium. Liturgies and acts of repentance are being planned around the slave trade, for example, which raise questions about the validity of one generation repenting on behalf of another, how forgiveness can possibly be given when the victims are long dead, and the part forgiveness has to play in reconciliation with the past and commitment to justice for the future.

From a planning meeting held in Coventry in July 1997, a series of principles of good practice for repentance liturgies emerges. These included:

(1)   to meet the relevant people to hear their story and discover if they want to be asked to forgive—care should be taken that the act of penitence is not prepared only by the oppressors, where this can be avoided;

(2)   to make sure that the liturgy does not make assumptions that all of the parties cannot share;

(3)   to tell the truth (which means recognizing that some victims have themselves oppressed others);

(4)   that we should not expect to resolve decades or centuries of injustice.

Of these, perhaps the last is most fundamentally important. The expectation of traditional liturgical practice is that resolution is the achievable aim. But it may be that some of the acts of repression, torture, destruction of culture and dehumanization must simply stand in history as finally unforgiveable acts.

Traditions Challenging Worshippers

Where Scripture is used in worship, and the worshipping community is enabled to encounter its stories, prophecies, teachings, poetry and imagery in complete freedom of dialogue, the text, itself challenged by the experience of the community, has the power to bring its own challenge to the worshipping body. We share what Ruether describes: 'when a text is used in liturgy it becomes more than an inspirational reading. It becomes a paradigmatic text. It becomes a place where we expect to encounter the transforming Spirit speaking to our own lives' (1985: 135). For this to happen, the way we encounter Scripture in worship has to change, and is changing.

Where change is taking place, approaches to scripture as sacred text in worship form a dynamic organic whole. Traditionally, Scripture has been segregated from liturgy in one of two ways. The 'lesson' or 'reading' isolates Scripture from other, more participative elements in worship, such as hymns or the liturgical dialogue. The congregation listens to Scripture and, no matter how carefully the worship leader draws theological links, or how well the passage is read, non-participation in the scriptural content of the service deprives the congregation of the chance to engage dynamically with the Bible itself. Of course, listening can be a participatory act, but presenting the Bible in the same, read, form week by week militates against creative engagement.

In another form of worship which has become traditional, Scripture is barely encountered at all. In certain contexts, congregations worship by means of songs and choruses, interspersed with fervent prayer, but in this case participation is carried to such an extent that the transcendent voice of Scripture and its ultimate challenge may not be heard. Encounter with the Bible is removed from worship altogether, to house groups and Bible studies which not all members of the congregation will attend.

There is a need, first of all, to enable congregations to bring their own living experiences into a dynamic interaction with the experiences told in Scripture. As this happens, the power to interpret Scripture is democratized, and passes out of the hands of the preacher or priest. The variety of interpretation increases and the range of Scripture used enlarges, because participants begin to explore for themselves. This happens not only in the context of the single group or congregation, but as experience is shared and, in particular, as the voices of different cultures are interwoven. By this means the lives of local groups or congregations are further enriched as new ways of experiencing and encountering Scripture give rise to further insights.

Perhaps the single most dramatic example of the enlarged range of Scripture is the liberation theologies' re-encounter with the Hebrew scriptures. Traditional worship has concentrated almost entirely on the New Testament. 'Old Testament lessons' are generally confined to a glorification of monarchy in Israel, a few messianic passages and carefully selected readings from the major prophets. In traditions where the psalms may be said or sung weekly, these are generally carefully expurgated for public worship. Pew Bibles may be New Testament only, or New Testament and Psalms, as are the Bibles left by the Gideons in hotel rooms or given to schoolchildren. Even the Bible Society 'Open Book' tapes for congregations, in response to the general fact that people do not read the Bible for themselves, only offer the New Testament.

The impression given is that the Hebrew scriptures are too difficult for most members of most congregations, and that they have nothing to say, except insofar as they are interpreted by the New Testament.

In stark contrast to this negative view, liberation theologies have discovered in the Hebrew scriptures a rich vein of spiritual and social experience which speaks directly to people who are oppressed and long for justice. The Hebrew people experienced oppression from both sides. They were slaves in Egypt and their own liturgical practices forbade them ever to forget that fact (Deut. 26.1–11). During their uncertain tenure of the land, they were frequently oppressed by their more powerful neighbours, and eventually exiled. The fact that a great part of Hebrew theological understanding is shaped by the two experiences of exodus and exile means that the experience of being oppressed speaks

from the heart of the Hebrew scriptures straight to the experience of
oppressed people.

But the Hebrew people were also oppressors. They entered the land
by means of the genocide of most of the indigenous tribes. They developed or copied a governmental system of despotic monarchy, which
amply fulfilled the misgivings of contemporary sources which resisted its
rise (e.g. Deut. 17.14-20; 1 Sam. 8).[2] While women are occasionally
shown as strong active participants in social and political life, they are
generally regarded as chattels and their part in the story is as 'wives,
harlots and concubines' (the title of Alice Laffey's book about the
women of the Hebrew Scriptures [1990]). Occasionally, they are treated
with breath-taking brutality.

Oppressed peoples therefore have two sources for encounter with a
similar experience in Scripture. They may find it in the experience of
the Hebrew people under slavery or in exile, or they may look to the
individuals and tribes who are oppressed by the Israelites. Indigenous
peoples whose land has been exploited by European invaders look to the
tribes who were forced out of the land. Robert Warrior writes:

> The obvious characters in the story for Native Americans to identify with
> are the Canaanites, the people who already lived in the promised land. As
> a member of the Osage Nation of American Indians who stands in soli-
> darity with other tribal people around the world, I read the Exodus sto-
> ries with Canaanite eyes. And, it is the Canaanite side of the story that has
> been overlooked by those seeking to articulate theologies of liberation.
> Especially ignored are those parts of the story that describe Yahweh's
> command to mercilessly annihilate the indigenous population (1997).

For women facing multiple discrimination on the grounds of race as
well as of gender, the figure of Hagar has become a focus of interpretation. Delores Williams writes that

> Christian womanist theologians…identify and reflect upon those biblical
> stories in which poor oppressed women had a special encounter with
> divine emissaries of God, like the spirit. In the Hebrew Testament,
> Hagar's story is most illustrative and relevant to Afro-American women's
> experience of bondage, of African heritage, of encounter with God/

---

2.   These are contemporary sources only inasmuch as they may contain contemporary elements. The Deuteronomistic writings are arguably much later in their
present form. However, they may well reflect attitudes of the time. It is clear that the
transition from charismatic to dynastic leadership was not smooth nor straightforward.

emissary in the midst of fierce, survival struggles. Kate Cannon among a number of black female preachers and ethicists urges black Christian women to regard themselves as Hagar's sisters (1989: 185).

Hagar is a powerful example, for she is not a victim, but a survivor. She is not 'a surrogate—one who suffers for humanity's sin. Rather she survived and her son grew to be a wild man who avenged the injustice done to his mother' (Hayes 1995: 57). Therefore she encourages us to survive, rather than to emulate the defeated victim, and calls us to long for and work for justice.

From this perspective, black Christian women can offer a challenge both to white women and to black Christians. Williams marks this double challenge: 'If womanist theological method is informed by a liturgical intent, then womanist theology will be relevant to (and will reflect) the thought, worship, and action of the black church with the discordant and prophetic messages emerging from womanist participation in multidialogics' (1989: 184). Therefore womanist theology is not derivative from nor subsumable under white feminist theology. On the other hand, 'a liturgical intent will also allow womanist theology to challenge the thought/worship/action of the black church with the discordant and prophetic messages emerging from scripture' (Williams 1989: 184).

The New Testament, with its short time-span, and fairly single-minded didactic intent, does not provide the space for this kind of reflection. It is in rediscovering the enormous range of material in the Hebrew scriptures, its rootedness in the history of communities, the interweaving of disparate and even, sometimes, contradictory view points, and the mature development of theology over hundreds of years and many generations, that liberation theologies have found not only new stories to tell, but a new way of telling the story.

Rosemary Radford Ruether recognizes this in her writing on women-church, when she writes: 'From our Hebrew heritage we particularly reclaim sensitivity to historical injustice and the longing for historical redemption that tended to be spiritualized or suppressed by a Christian misinterpretation of the belief in a salvation already embodied in a Christ in the past' (1985: 104). Alongside the glorification of a despotic monarchy, and triumphalism over possession of a land won by divine genocide, which is undoubtedly there in the Hebrew scriptures, there is a continuous tradition of dissent from the abuse of power.

This prophetic tradition arises in opposition to the concentration of power in a dynastic and unaccountable monarchy. King David's story shows him gradually succumbing to the seductions of despotic power, and accompanied in that process by the warnings of the prophet Nathan. When he desires to cloister God in a purpose-built temple, it is Nathan who reminds him of the nomadic roots and pilgrim ideals of the people of Israel and their God (2 Sam. 7.1-16). When he commits adultery with Bathsheba and murders her husband, it is Nathan who highlights the horrific injustice of what he has done (2 Sam. 12.1-14).

Throughout the period of the monarchy, the prophets are constant in upholding the rights of the powerless and oppressed. Amos and Hosea speak out against the excesses of the northern kingdom before the exile of the eighth century; Isaiah and Jeremiah and, to a lesser degree, Ezekiel, condemn the inequalities of the southern kingdom during the following 150 years. There is an argument that the process was actually continuous, in that the prophecy of Hosea's tradition may have been preserved after the fall of the northern kingdom and formed the basis of the Deuteronomistic reform which led to the rediscovery of the book of the law in the Temple (2 Kgs 22.8). After the return from exile, the Isaiah tradition continued to call for a society based on justice and equality rather than a return to the inequalities of the past (Isa. 58; 61.1-6; 65.17-25).

Besides the overt prophetic call to justice, there exist stories of victims, preserved within even the most triumphal of traditions, as if to puncture their arrogant certainty. Tamar's horrifying abuse is part of the narrative, parallel to David's mighty conquests, of the slow self-destruction of this dysfunctional family. The cost of David's self-centred power-seeking is borne by his fractured family—a familiar story.

The prophets and the survivors show us a fresh way of reading the story of Jesus. It is extraordinary how the life and teachings of Jesus have been subsumed in traditional liturgical practice under the significance of his birth, death and resurrection. Most major hymnbooks have large sections on the birth of Jesus (Advent and Christmas), and equally large sections devoted to the events leading up to and including his death and resurrection (Holy Week, Good Friday and Easter). Sandwiched in the middle of all this is a section on his life and teachings. This, of course, is the emphasis of the epistles, which draw their teachings about Christian living from other sources, and focus on Jesus mainly as the Christ, a theological symbol for the salvation of the world and the conquest of death.

The *Methodist Hymn Book* (1933) has 190 hymns under the section 'The Lord Jesus Christ', of which 28 are under the subsection 'His life, teaching and ministry'. In the same tradition, but 50 years later, *Hymns and Psalms* has 205 hymns under 'The Eternal Word', of which 29 fall into subsections to do with the life and teachings of Jesus. The balance in other books, even more recently, is much the same. The worshipping life of the churches focuses on the person and work of Christ, rather than the life and teachings of Jesus.

But the Gospels record a radical set of teachings, which draws on the call for justice and a radically new society found in the prophets. As has been seen, Jesus quotes Isaiah 61 and may have based substantial teaching on this passage. Many of his parables are pointed denials of privilege and status. He denounces the hypocrisy of the religious professionals with bitter and biting satire (Mt. 23) and speaks quite offensively about the kind of people who will be invited to the great feast when the expected guests are too arrogant to come (Mt. 22.1-14). By mixing with and touching people who were the outcasts of his day, Jesus overturned the great taboos which, to their great shame, the churches still uphold. The woman with the flow of blood, the loose-living Samaritan, the untouchable leper, the despised child, are not only addressed by Jesus but are set at the centre of his new and radical theology.

By ignoring the teachings and demeanour of Jesus, the Christian tradition has managed to create a spiritualized faith, based on a dualism which enables the call for justice to be totally sidelined. Much of our worship is addressed to the Christ of the epistles, raised up, divine, out of this world and consequently rendered safe. The divine Christ can save individuals out of the world, but he can't change the world as it is. Worshippers are encouraged to exult in their own spirituality, to glory in their own salvation, deaf to the hard words that Jesus is actually reported as speaking.

If the radical message of Scripture is to be heard, our encounter with these scriptures as sacred texts through liturgy must interact with the historical reality of our communities and lives. Ruether again: 'For Women-Church, entry into messianic community means, particularly, conversion from patriarchy as ideology and social system. It means the formation of a critical culture and community of liberation from patriarchy. It means our nurture and growth in our new and true humanity as women, and as women and men together' (1985: 108). This is a tremendously exciting reality. Christian communities willing to be shaped by the transforming Spirit of Scripture find a wholly new sense of freedom and renewal. It comes out again and again in the literature, for example in the description of an Asian church, which, 'celebrates with joy, in symbol and song, in rite and dance, its own life and its hope of the new life to which it struggles to give birth' (Perera 1995: 51), or the message from the seminar, 'Women in Dialogue: Wholeness of Vision towards the 21st Century' (May 1994, Bossey, Geneva): 'We have had a foretaste of the church of the future in our daily worship together. Celebration, local diversity, local ways of prayer and music, mutual conversation about Scripture—in meditation and praise we were one community embodied in our diversity and worshipping God, the Source of Life' (Ortega 1995: 177).

Communal worship and the life of the community are wholly interdependent. Without expression in the life of the community, liturgy is no better than superstitious practice, words and actions engaged in to appease the deity whose anger the injustices condoned in the community rightly arouse. Without liturgical or symbolic corporate activity, the life of the community has no space for reflection and may become fragmented. By retelling the sacred stories, celebrating and mourning together, the community gathers the wisdom and strength to bring about change. Ruether finds that, 'Most church liturgies are dead precisely because they have no real reference point in a community that has a collective sense of its identity and a social praxis that expresses that identity' (1985: 92).

I can comment on this from the experience of my own Christian community, where encounter with Scripture has led to active involvement in an inner-city community. Our radical Christian stance affects the arts policy of the secular organization which has been set up by the congregation to organize events in the building in which the church worships. Two large spaces are made available specifically to marginalized communities for performance arts, and therefore the building becomes a microcosm of the multi-cultural community of Islington, including performances and audiences drawn from a variety of ethnic backgrounds, from able-bodied people and people with disabilities, and across the age spectrum. Further engagement with Scripture drove the congregation to open part of the building to homeless people and drives that same congregation constantly to ensure that contact between the different communities, including the church itself, is as free from paternalism and hostility as possible, and that women's voices are heard within all the communities that use the building. Therefore we have to find ways of challenging, for example, the racism of many homeless people and the misogyny of some cultural groups.

Our patterns of worship cannot remain untouched by living out a radical theology in the community. By a continuous process, the worshipping life of my Christian community has changed. New worship material has enriched our liturgy, with new hymns replacing some of the triumphalistic or patriarchal hymns of the past. Dance, discussion and visual imagery play a larger part in our worship, though, as with engagement with communities, the temptation is to drift continuously back to older, 'safer' ways.

If such transformation is possible in a local community, where encounter with Scripture in worship challenges and changes established patterns which then reflect back on the way in which Scripture is encountered, then interaction in worship beyond the local congregation may enrich and encourage the change that is possible. While radical congregations often find themselves isolated in their own immediate locale, there are opportunities for sharing of ideas and experience in worship.

The journal *Worship Live*, and other similar publications, form along networks of people engaged in creating and using worship material of a radical nature. The so-called 'alternative church year', including Sundays with a special emphasis on themes such as homelessness, unemployment and racial justice offer opportunities for congregations to reflect liturgically on issues of importance to the struggle for justice. These Sundays are seen by some as an irrelevant excrescence on an otherwise adequate liturgical year. But they have had a subtle effect on the nature of worship. By introducing justice issues to large numbers of ordinary congregations, as proper content for worshipping together, they have altered the relationship between worship and life for a large part of the Church in Britain. They have also opened up opportunities for writers who produce material which is based on other than lectionary passages of scripture to gain a hearing.

Where networks or gatherings enable it to happen, there is a sharing of material, worship experience and exegesis. There is a sense of real excitement as worshipping groups learn from each other. Separate groups may find it impossible to make powerful links between prophetic worship and action in the community but, together, we may bring the promised community to reality, at least from time to time.

Chapter Four

Deep Calls to Deep

Liturgical Development

Perhaps the most powerful setting for liturgical development is outside the regular worshipping community in collective worship at large or small gatherings. The quadrennial Ecumenical Forum of European Christian Women (EFECW) and, more recently, the European Women's Synod and its related national Women's Synods offer great opportunities for creative acts of worship. These, and similar gatherings, also allow room for tensions between communities to arise in the context of worship.

At the European Women's Synod in Gmünden in 1996, a group of women read the passage from Luke's Gospel about the importunate widow and the unjust judge. The act of worship took place in a court-yard with a well in the centre. The well was dressed with red cloth, representing the judge. The passage was read several times in different languages. After each reading, the participants joined in a dance, and were invited to name injustices known to them. The dance travelled around the well, but always came back to where it began, symbolizing the often fruitless persistence of women against injustice.

Like the Synod, the EFECW meeting gave many opportunities for experimental worship. At the start of one day, the participants were sitting in the hall, in two blocks with a central aisle. The people sitting along the aisle on both sides were invited to stand and face each other across the aisle in two long lines holding hands with their backs to the two blocks. A clown danced into the room and smiled at the seated participants. She danced up to the 'wall' of backs and mimed distress at not being able to communicate with the people on the other side. After a while, she danced to the front of the aisle and took the hands of the people either side of the aisle at the front. She then drew them with her as she danced between the two lines. As the lines followed her, they were reversed and turned to face the two blocks. The clown then introduced them to the seated participants, and danced and laughed with both sides.

At the 1998 Forum of EFECW in El Exorial, Spain, tension exploded between some Western European women who found the use of exclusive language in worship intolerable and some Russian Orthodox women who found their position compromised by the use of female imagery for God. Both groups expressed anger, and suggested that their continued presence at the Forum was in doubt. The Western European women were hurt and angered by being expected to use words like 'Lord' (Seigneur, Herr) which trapped them in a patriarchal spirituality. They could not retain their integrity as radical Christians. For the Russian Orthodox women, the situation was different. Their faith community held gatherings such as the EFECW in deep suspicion and those women had taken specific risks in order to be there. A radical stance on the part of EFECW rendered their participation even more vulnerable than it already was. They were not only shocked as individuals by female imagery of God; their integrity with their faith community was threatened.

Similarly, worship at this kind of event has evoked challenges from lesbian women, from women with disabilities and from black women. A worshipping community which is seeking to challenge exclusivity at one point is rightly challenged by others excluded by it. While the process is sharp and focused at a major gathering, it also forms part of the kind of networking which goes on through publications. When I have confronted groups in churches, students unions and workshops with some of the diversity of worship material in *Worship Live*, the response has sometimes been hostile, often provoking intense discussion, with the same kind of potential for the recognition of marginalized groups within the discussion process.

In every group which expresses horror at the unrestrained anger of the Christian Survivors of Sexual Abuse firework service (see p. 93), there will be one or two people who are themselves survivors or have other similar experiences, who will require room for their sense of rejection by the mainstream view of the group.

One annual service which manages to hold together a traditional constituency and yet introduce radical ideas is what is still known in

England as the Women's World Day of Prayer, though in other parts of the world the word 'Women's' has been dropped. Founded as a service to bind the fellowship of women with missionaries in different parts of the world, it has maintained a global perspective.

The traditional closing hymn, 'The Day thou Gavest, Lord, Is Ended', is a reminder of its past, and is sung with enormous affection even today. Each year, the service is prepared by a group of women in a different part of the world. The concerns of the 'host' country are detailed in a foreword to the order of service which is supplied to each member of each congregation, and there is generally an attempt to engage with its culture. In 1996, the service was put together in Haiti, and Christian Aid produced complementary material, including a tremendously moving image of a grieving woman.

The introduction to that service included the following information: 'Women play a very important part in Haitian society. They are the mainstay of both domestic and economic life. Because of this, in recent years, physical and sexual violence have been used against them as a form of political repression.' This is picked up in a prayer of supplication, using the Haitian word 'Anm'wé', which means, 'look out!' The congregation shouts 'Anm'wé' loudly between petitions for children 'who are victims of hunger, injustice and oppression', for those who 'are cut down from their earliest years because they dare to claim their most fundamental rights', and for the people who 'look for food in rubbish piles', whose 'immediate surroundings are filth and stench'.

Services in other years have invited participants to engage in symbolic acts: anointing with oil, sharing in a feast, dancing the offering, and so on. Year by year, the concerns and liturgical riches of single nations are shared around the world. This rather despised and overlooked annual service is promoting change right at the heart of traditional church life.

Multiplicity

In a postmodern society, it is more acceptable for diverse and even contradictory theological standpoints to exist together without the necessity for a 'truth' to affirm one and condemn the other. I suggested earlier that rediscovery of the Hebrew scriptures was in part the rediscovery of a theological diversity which was not possible within the confines of the New Testament. For example, in the return from exile, it is quite clear that the liberal and inclusive Isaianic tradition is in direct conflict with the exclusiveness of the Ezekiel tradition. Ezekiel's exclusivity is shown precisely in the field of worship, as he seeks to restrict access to worship to the chosen, 'racially pure' people of Israel, and the priesthood to a group of people who are both racially and religiously uncontaminated (Ezek. 44.9-16). The Temple and its ritual is central. Isaiah, on the other hand, opens access to worship, and even approach to the altar, to all (Isa. 56.1-8) and ultimately questions the very existence of the Temple and its sacrificial ritual (66.1-3). For the Isaianic tradition, the governing principle is not purity but justice. The new community is based on equality rather than hierarchy.

While there are still many people in the Ezekiel tradition in the churches, there is a model in the Isaiah tradition for a far more open approach. Worship can be the most exclusive of human activities, but it need not be. It is possible that the arena of worship may give room for diversity to take shape as process, allowing anger and hurt as well as reconciliation and hope to be expressed.

Something of this kind happened at the conference to mark the end of the Decade for the Churches in Solidarity with Women, at Durham in the spring of 1998. There was a choice of morning worship, colour-coded as follows: yellow for light, life, spring, sun, resurrection—traditional morning worship; red for anger, passion, love—a noisy service with singing and symbolic action; green for hope, environment, nurture—planned as an outdoor service (though it rained); blue for water, sky—a service of quiet meditation; purple for shadows, darkness, mystery—a period of silence, using incense. As people could choose their 'mood' and style, conflict was avoided. The following morning, however, we met conflict head on as we faced the problem of eucharistic hospitality. In a gathering of women and some men, including church leaders as well as representatives of feminist groups, diversity could be contained where there was choice, but we had to express our inability to share, and our grief where choice gave way to a wider community.

Linda A. Moody explores the efficacy of worship as a conductor of diversity in *Women and Theology*. She begins from the possibility that, 'in our praxis of solidarity, committed Christian womanist, mujerista, Asian American and white feminist liberationist theologians might do well to even worship with each other and pray together' (Moody 1994: 195). In the context of worship, she says, we may glimpse a 'multi-world view' in which large and small diversities form a nexus for unexpected revelations and liberation. It is hard to accept diversity of culture. Janet Morley found this in her compilation for Christian Aid, *Bread of Tomorrow* (1992). The actual words of the poor and excluded are sometimes offensively triumphalistic to the ears of the rich who are in the process of eschewing triumphalism. She comments, 'We should feel uneasy with a lusty singing of the poor, when we have no right to triumphalism given where we are standing and whose side we are in fact on' (Morley 1992: 4).

Ann O'Hara Graff takes this further. Reflecting on the theory of a 'polycentric church' in the writings of Roberto Goizueta, a Hispanic theologian, she notes three issues: 'that diversity is not to be misunderstood as individualism, bereft of institution and tradition'; 'that authentic pluralism demands that all contributors to the common conversation be full partners, not voices already interpreted by groups in dominant positions'; and that the aim is 'conversation, not mere equivocity' (O'Hara Graff 1994: 209).

The first of these is fundamentally important to the attitude with which voices are heard. Discordant views can be dismissed as long as they are seen as individual aberrations or, better still, representative of prejudged and despised viewpoints. In worship, however, where stories are remembered and individuals stand in their own spiritual and communal tradition, mere dismissal ought not to be possible. Recognition of the authority of each individual as a representative and product of a complex interaction of traditions should form a natural part of the process of communal worship.

Of course, this is not the case, because dominant voices inevitably tend to take over the process. O'Hara Graff pictures the alternative as a process where there is no longer any centre to create margins for the marginalized. She says, 'For those who have had dominant public voices to yield to those who are now speaking as equals, is a major step, as is the step to own one's voice when it has been denied or suppressed' (O'Hara Graff 1994: 210).

Something of this is present in new ways of thinking about mission, in which 'partnership' has become a theological and practical model, replacing the imperialistic paternalism which shaped European mission over the last 200 years or more. The struggle to stop seeing Europe, Britain, England or even London as the centre and the non-European world as the 'field' has been instructive. The fact that most missionary agencies' headquarters are located in Europe means that new patterns face a continual battle with geography.

In the Council for World Mission, the process began in the 1970s with a conscious redefinition of the old London Missionary Society as a global partnership, with resources of different kinds located in each partner church. As the concept of the centre dissolved, 'sending' missionaries, mostly from the northern hemisphere to the south, was replaced by the concept of sharing personnel, now in previously unthinkable directions—south to north (e.g. Samoa to Britain) and south to south (e.g. Botswana to Guyana).

But there were unforeseen implications. Other suppressed voices, which no one had even thought of, began to plead for a hearing. Within all the member churches, it was male leaders who attended conferences, took part in theological discussions and made decisions about the use of resources. When the call went out for 30% leading to 50% female participation in these areas of power, many of the partner churches, whose voices had been loud in condemnation of Euro-centrism, were vociferous in support of androcentrism.

A more complex reaction was the tendency for formerly dependent church bodies in the Pacific Islands or South America not to share the British theologians' enthusiasm for equal partnership, and there were long struggles to overcome a 'dependency culture'—a practical version of O'Hara Graff's 'step to own one's voice when it has been denied or suppressed'. It appeared that people who had for so long been on the margins had come to identify themselves in that respect. Hannah Ward and Jennifer Wild describe the phenomenon in *Guard the Chaos* (1995a). They question the place of the 'margins' as the place for the prophet, the victim, the oppressed, the creative, the eccentric. They write, ' "Being on the margins" has become a vocation for some. It is certainly more often than not the place of the self-styled martyr' (Ward and Wild 1995a: 29). They go on, 'To define oneself as marginal is to define oneself in relation to someone else's centre; it is to accept another's definition of how things are' (Ward and Wild 1995a: 30).

In place of the concept of 'margins' they prefer the image of the threshold and the concept of liminality: 'To be *between* here and there is to live in the faith that there is a future', that is, it suggests process from old, oppressive ways to new ways, of which the liminal person or group is the prophet.

A philosophical framework for this kind of non-centralized diversity can be found in 'process thought', the system devised by Alfred North

Whitehead. Whitehead was a mathematician, writing during the first half of the twentieth century, at the time when great advances were being made in mathematical theory. His aim was to work out a view of the universe which took account of first relativity theory and then quantum theory.

The traditional materialistic view of the universe would not stand up to the discovery that space and time formed a continuum. The universe did not consist of objects existing in space through time, but of events taking place in space and time. These events were involved in a series of causal sequences, so that each event was influenced by many other events in its past and, in turn, influenced a whole multiplicity of events in the future.

For Whitehead, then, the universe was governed not by dualism, but by multiplicity and unity. Each event was a gathering together of multiple influence into a unity, which then became part of another multiplicity of events with a causal effect on the future. The easiest kind of event for human beings to understand is a moment of human life. At each moment, human beings perceive their world in ways that are partially defined by their past. They make movements, responses or decisions which have immediate or long-term effects on their own future and that of others.

But moments of human life form an infinitesimally small proportion of the events which make up the universe. By far the majority of events are not known about by humans, and the process of the universe goes forward without reference to human agency or perception.

The 'point of view' of each event is called a standpoint. It is the universe as seen from the perspective of that event. So human beings have standpoints from which they make responses and decisions, summing up the past and affecting the future. But every event has a standpoint as well. It does not require conscious perception. The process which is reality gathers itself into standpoints which are unities of the multiplicity of events, and which form the basis for the continuance of process. Because we are human, we think of standpoints as human perceptions, but Whitehead's philosophy is not anthropocentric, and any confluence of events may be a standpoint.

Two things are important in this context. First, standpoints are single points in a continuum of experience. They are always an interweaving of the immediate and long-term past, and each standpoint becomes part of the past which is consequently interwoven into a new set of standpoints. Secondly, standpoints are, by definition, many and diverse. There is no single, true or universal standpoint from which the true picture of the whole universe, or even the story so far, can be seen.

There is not even one single divine standpoint which remains unchanged, and to which worshippers aspire. For Whitehead, God is fully immanent in the process and shares each standpoint: God, 'shares with every new creation its actual world' (Whitehead 1979: 523).

God's transcendence lies in the elements of purpose. A standpoint relates not only to the past, but to the future. Every standpoint is moving towards a future which is consequent on choices made from that standpoint. Choices made from a standpoint that includes damage and hurt from the past may be further damaging and hurtful for the future. They may carry destructiveness as a purpose. But for Whitehead, God's existence in the fabric of events is as a 'lure' towards creativity and perfection (even perfection, by the way, is not permanent, but a perfection may need to be broken down so that a greater perfection may come to being).

God shares each standpoint, then, but not as a neutral observer. God is the longing for healing, the hope for a better future, the carrier of inspiration and creativity from the past to the future: 'This final phase of God's nature is ever enlarging itself. In it the complete adjustment of the immediacy of joy and suffering reaches the final end of creation. This end is existence in the perfect unity of adjustment as means, and in the perfect multiplicity of attainment of individual types of self-existence' (Whitehead 1979: 531-52). Remember that perfection is itself in process, and it becomes clear that Whitehead is not talking about an eschaton—the end of the world and a heaven not to be achieved in this world. He uses, 'final end' in a teleological sense—the final purpose, the end as the goal towards which God and the world are striving.

This philosophy provides a framework for the kinds of discussion of worship quoted in this chapter. There is no fundamental 'norm' by which worshippers are judged. They do not have to pretend to be living perfect lives, or to hold opinions which conform with doctrine or dogma. On the other hand, there is the opportunity for change, for metanoia, both individual and communal, in which God's lure towards creativity and perfection engages with the worshipping community in healing, challenge, inspiration and hope. The outcome can then be healed lives, or lives which are beginning to be open to healing; readiness for reconciliation or the recognition that forgiveness must be withheld in holy anger; affirmed longing for and commitment to justice.

In an act of worship, each person participates from his or her own standpoint, and their contribution will be the richer if that standpoint is acknowledged and accepted. If a worshipping community is open to change based on the enrichment brought to it by the diversity of participants, those participants will be able to recognize God's lure in the community at large, and will be ready to participate in healing and justice wherever God's lure calls them on. So worshipping life may be intertwined with a renewal or severing of personal relationships, or engagement in a local community project, or involvement in global issues. God's creativity, encountered in the worshipping community, will bring about change at some level, which both affects the individual and allows the individual to participate creatively in the community.

Metanoia and Change

This is a long way from the dead liturgies that Ruether perceives and describes as divorced from the collective identity and praxis of a community. For it to be possible, the language, the ambience and the conduct of worship must cease to constrict participation. But the process from dead liturgies to the full creative potential of worship is long and can be painful for those who embrace it as well as those who are left behind. The change needs to embrace everything about worship. Nelle Morton, writing in Christ's and Plaskow's (1992), *Womanspirit Rising*, records her frustration during the 1970s, when language was changing, but symbolism remained rooted in patriarchal culture. She writes, 'we are saying no to those images, symbols, structures, and practices which cripple us and keep us from claiming our rightful personhood. We are saying no to a system that legitimates these images through cosmic myths, language, and daily dramas of etiquette' (Morton 1992: 159).

She struggles with the vision of what a truly inclusive celebration could be like.

> One can only speculate on what celebration could be were mutuality (love) possible in the community of faith; were the oppressed of the earth trusted to be a valid part of that community./It may be that the most authentic celebration is not that which can be structured from above—not that as considered by the control group proper for the oppressed... Maybe the most authentic celebration begins with rejoicing in that which is breaking up from down under (1992: 165).

This, above all, is the experience of authentic worship, that it is not imposed by authority—indeed, it struggles with the whole notion of authority—but it arises from telling the stories of the oppressed. Women's stories are stories of oppressed people, but women as oppressors need to listen as well, to hear the stories of people they have oppressed.

When the standpoint of the participants is the starting-point of worship, a radically new kind of liturgy is possible. From the standpoint of their own experience, worshippers can begin to interact with the stories of tradition, the words, actions and symbols of worship and the sacred Scripture. New words, actions and symbols will arise and begin to form new interweavings of tradition; and old traditions will be re-interpreted, taking on new significance, or rejected. Sometimes it is the recognition of the destructive power of an old, but well-loved tradition, and its rejection, which causes the most pain.

But the starting-point has to shift. No amount of tinkering with words and symbols will bring worship to life if the majority of the participants form a passive, powerless audience. In a whole variety of different places and cultures, sometimes in the context of a traditional church, and sometimes in gatherings of 'refugees' from traditional churches, worshipping communities have experimented with this shift of power.

The story is told again and again. At the World Council of Churches Manila Consultation in 1985, liturgy included, 'God-talk', which was discussion enabled by the use of murals and by the adoption of an equalizing position—the participants all sat on the floor (Mananzan 1995: 31). Among Korean women's organizations, a story-telling ministry arose (Lee-Park 1995: 44). In 1992, in Latin America, a gathering of women theologians marked the five-hundredth anniversary of Columbus's arrival. They were African, indigenous and gypsy women. 'It was a meeting of equals—women from different religious traditions sharing together, listening with respect to one another and celebrating the cosmos' (de Oliveira 1995: 68).

In London, a group of women, disaffected with the Church of England because of its slowness to change, began to meet under the banner of 'The St Hilda Community'. Their story is illustrative of much of the experience of new worshipping communities. There was excitement, development, renewal, a sense that something genuinely new was emerging. But there were also conflicts, particularly in the struggle over issues of leadership and authority.

Their starting-point was both simple and ambitious. They wanted 'to design a radical new way of being Church. We did not want to give up our Christian allegiance, still less to found a sect. But we wanted a form of worship—"non-sexist liturgy" as we soon began to call it, that gave full space and authority to women, without apology, secrecy or shame' (Furlong 1991: 6).

The power shift was essential to the new forms of worship. Sitting in a circle, participants were encouraged to offer 'ministry' as they felt able to: 'Ministry is multifaceted; therefore, that area to which one person feels called one week may change the next week. Primary, however, is the fact that each person actively engages in some form of ministry each time they are present. This ministry could range from facilitating the overall pattern of worship, to dancing, to participating in intercessions, to creative listening' (Furlong 1991: 19). Shared leadership gave rise to creativity, enabling participants to find and exercise their own gifts: 'Those who had never written a prayer or shaped a liturgy before were surprised at how much more deeply they had to think about it, what new insights they acquired into the purpose of worship, and the sort of drama that was needed to make it come alive' (Furlong 1991: 9).

As participants brought their own life-experiences to worship, symbols began to be used in new and creative ways: ancient symbols, such as grapes, yeast, oil, water, incense, and new ones. The writers describe a Palm Sunday liturgy in which forsythia branches were passed round the circle. Each worshipper stripped off some of the bloom until,

> The denuded branches, empty of new growth and flowers, were placed back in the centre of the circle for contemplation. As we each realised our potential for destroying the Tree of Life, we were humbled by our failure to receive Christ and by our power to tear the Christ energy from other human beings. Many women also connected this symbolic act with the ways in which they, as images of God incarnate, had been violated (Fageol 1991: 22).

Significantly, the symbol did not 'mean' something definite. It was not a way of getting some well-formed doctrine across to a congregation. Instead, it became a way of releasing meaning in the worshippers. The bare branches were potent, the destructive act connected with the women's experience of destroying and being destroyed. Strong images from tradition were invoked, the tree of life, the Incarnation and imago Dei. But the direction of interpretation was from the 'bottom up'. The participants' experience interpreted both symbol and tradition. The symbol was intended not to impose teaching about the tree of life, for example, but to open a way for the ancient image to interact with present experience.

Interaction of this kind becomes sacramental, where the symbol embodies both the divine and the experience of the worshipper so that the divine becomes present to the worshipping community in the liturgical act. Churches have defined two or seven sacraments, depending on the tradition of the church. Some traditions hold no sacramental services, regarding the actions of common life as the proper setting for God to break through in sacramental ways. The Salvation Army and Religious Society of Friends (Quakers) hold this view. Of the two sacraments common to most traditions, it is the eucharist that focuses issues in inclusive worship.

Again, the experience of the St Hilda Community is instructive, since the community was formed in direct response to the issue of women's ordination in the Church of England. One of the central issues was whether and how the community could engage in eucharistic worship. As it was not an Anglican community, though most of its members were in fact Anglican and it had arisen out of an Anglican concern, it could draw on the eucharistic practices of other traditions. Before women were ordained in the Church of England, eucharistic hospitality allowed its members to receive communion from ministers of other churches in full communion with it, many of whom would have been women, as women had been ordained in many of the free churches for a considerable period. Therefore, ministers of free churches were occasionally invited to preside at eucharistic worship in the community.

There were also women ordained in other parts of the Anglican communion. Suzanne Fageol, an ordained priest in the Episcopal Church in the USA, and herself a dynamic radical thinker, began to conduct eucharists at the St Hilda Community. These were, of course, illegal, in a way that the ministry of Free Church women was not, and raised all sorts of issues. The community invited Suzanne to be its priest. In accepting, Suzanne jeopardized her own standing in the Church of England. She also struggled with her own principles of 'equality between women and men, clergy and laity' (Fageol 1991: 17). Both Suzanne and the community struggled with the concept of her being the priest of a community which shared responsibility for liturgical practice among its members.

Of course, the illegal celebration of the eucharist eventually came to the attention of the media. The St Hilda services had always been public and had been advertised. There was no attempt to hide them. Monica Furlong recalls the build up to a famous occasion when Suzanne Fageol celebrated the eucharist in the car park of St Benet's from which the community had been evicted after failing to give an undertaking not to celebrate the eucharist. Prior to the occasion, media pressure had intensified. Monica recalls, 'I remember being rung up at two in the morning... Suzanne was virtually under siege—she telephoned once, in some panic, to say that her front garden was full of photographers' (Furlong 1991: 13).

The eucharist was conducted under a blaze of TV lights, and with a considerable police presence. Monica Furlong again: '"Why are you here?" I asked one [policeman]. "In case there's any trouble", he replied grimly, "fighting and that sort of thing", and then, splendidly missing the point, "But don't you worry, dear. We'll protect you"' (1991: 13).

Undoubtedly, the courage and intelligent actions of the St Hilda Community were instrumental both in bringing women's ordination in the Church of England about, and in preparing for what that experience would be like. Monica Furlong concludes, 'we hope that our existence has made it harder for the churches to condescend to women, and for women to collude with that process. Then we shall not have struggled in vain' (1991: 15). But the community has achieved much more than that. Because of the St Hilda Community and other experimental groups, women's ministry has a background of experimental worship patterns. Unlike churches in which women were ordained early and without fuss, the Church of England created a milieu of discussion (at best) and exclusion (at worst) in which the very concept of ministry was under scrutiny, and traditional patterns of worship were questioned. This has had a beneficial effect on the ministry of women and the development of experiments in worship throughout the Christian community.

For women from the Protestant churches, whose worship is largely word-based, and rather despises ritual and imagery, the experience of ritualistic experimental worship has been tremendously enriching. For women of a Catholic tradition, there has been a rediscovery of rites that could bring women's experience into the church, when in fact they serve to repress women at every level of their existence. The debate over the ordination of women raised, for example, the ancient taboo against menstruating women. The idea of receiving communion from a menstruating priest was abhorrent to some opponents, revealing a deep-seated fear of female mystery and fecundity.

Celebrating Women's Experience

Rosemary Radford Ruether traces this particular taboo from its roots in the Hebrew literature.

> Menstruation has been turned by patriarchal religion into a source and symbol of the marginalisation of women from sacred power. Menstruating women were regarded as ritually taboo in Judaism. Remnants of this idea were restored in Eastern Orthodox and Medieval Christianity to suggest that the menstruating woman should refrain from Eucharist (that is, of course, from receiving it), and that women's generic pollution forbids them to enter the sanctuary or touch holy objects. This taboo lives on in secular myths that menstruating women are weak and irrational, and that their instability prohibits women from exercising responsible roles of power (1985: 217-18).

Women have, by and large, colluded in promulgating the myth. A girl's menarche is regarded as something of a curse—something that ties you down for the foreseeable future—while the menopause is regarded, paradoxically, as the loss of womanhood. These important moments in a woman's life are given no ritual significance in the life of the Christian community. Instead, girlhood, virginity and innocence are ritualized, and womanhood is vilified as unclean. There is no model for mature womanhood in the worshipping life of the Church, as there is for men, who will be leaders and for whom manhood is modelled in Christ and fatherhood in God.

The only traditional ritual which touches the experience of women is the 'churching' of women after the birth of a child, though this is no longer practised in the Roman Catholic Church, and exists with an emphasis on thanksgiving in the Anglican Church. Here again, women are regarded as unclean following an experience which connects with fertility. The ritual is quite definitely a purification rite, re-admitting the woman to the communicant body. Unchurched women were considered unlucky in the supersition of the community, with the ability to bring bad luck on others. A woman who was too ill, following the birth of her baby, to be churched, might be excluded from the baptism of her own child.

Natalie Knödel notes that the element of purification was exacerbated in the case of an illegitimate birth, in which case, the mother, 'was forced to repent in front of the whole congregation, preferably on a Sunday when a large congregation could be expected, before she could be churched' (1997: 117). The father of the child was not called upon to repent.

In the face of all this—their total invisibility in the rituals, language and identity of the worshipping community, and the defilement of all their proper functions—mature women have recently sought other ways of expressing their life in liturgical practice. While Knödel recognizes the deep-seated misogyny at the heart of the patriarchal ceremony of 'churching', she finds, in some of the ways it was adapted in earlier communities and has been adapted in more recent rites, a continuing tradition honouring womanhood on which feminist liturgists can build. The old tradition was used by women to focus on the new mother's experience in the light of the experience of other women. There was the opportunity for feasting, and a gathering of women friends, which was sometimes more important than the church ritual. Knödel sees the value of this, as it focuses not on the child, but on the woman, 'and her need to work out the experiences of pregnancy, the process of birth and her new role as mother' (1997: 122). She quotes new rites which take this, rather than purification, as their emphasis: for example, the 'Thanksgiving for the gift of a child' from the Uniting Church in Australia.

Hannah Ward's and Jennifer Wild's book, *Human Rites* (1995b), is a deliberately uncritical repository of liturgies around all manner of life experiences. The purpose of the book, they say, is, 'to provide a collection of services and rituals that demonstrate "liturgy from the ground up" ' (1995b: 1).

As well as naming ceremonies for babies, there is a celebration for the process of birth itself, which includes Kathy Galloway's recasting of the seven days of creation as seven times in the labour of love, which is birth. Recognizing that a pregnancy is not always successful and joyous, there are services of healing for a miscarriage and rituals for stillbirth and the death of a baby, and rituals surrounding abortion, which are intensely moving, since this act is either deeply disapproved of or entirely unmentioned in most Christian communities. One ritual has three movements: Preparation, the need for courage; During, the need for support; and After, guilt, the need for forgiveness, when her friends wash the woman, saying, 'We wash you with water as a symbol of the tears of mourning, the forgiveness of guilt, and the beginning of new life for you' (Vienna Cobb Anderson in Ward and Wild 1995b: nos. 76, 152).

Women's subjection to violence, abuse and rape are recognized in rituals which express anger against the perpetrators, and against the society that colludes in violence against women. Indeed, there is a great deal of anger, as well as joy, in many of these liturgies. This is welcome, since there is almost no opportunity to express anger in the traditional worship of the Church.

The passage from age to age of womanhood is also honoured, with a ritual to celebrate the passage from girlhood to young woman by Erice Fairbrother, and 'For my daughters, a liturgy for the celebration of your menarche', compiled by Sue Newman with words from Janet Morley and a blessing by Liz Campbell from the Greenham Common Agape. In both, the life-giving flow of blood is honoured, and celebration includes the drinking of red wine, which is symbolic of blood, and of maturity, as a 'grown-up' drink.

There are no services in this collection to mark the menopause, but there is a ritual for a woman's retirement, in which she says, 'All my life, I have walked and run after wisdom. Now I claim Wisdom's company for the rest of my life. How gracious is Wisdom!' and the co-celebrants respond, 'How gracious is Wisdom!'

Wisdom was also taken as the model for mature womanhood in a celebration drawn up to mark the fiftieth birthday of seven members of the Catholic Women's Network in the North-East of England. This ritual included readings about Wisdom from Ecclesiasticus and Baruch, and a years of wisdom circle. For the latter, the women all joined hands in a circle. Each woman spoke out her age, and a calculation was made of the years of wisdom present. They came to a little over 500 years.

Common symbols to many of these liturgies are candles, wine and anointing, which have a long history in the Christian tradition. There are also symbols drawn from the emerging rediscovery of Celtic spirituality, with an emphasis on the holiness of the created world. Mary Grey describes a ceremony which she devised with a group of women ordinands in Lichfield at a retreat before their ordination. A rite of passage ended with the ordinands burying seeds of bitterness in a bowl of earth and eating the grapes from which the seeds had been taken. Many chose to speak about the bitterness they wanted to leave behind, though for some it was so real that they wanted to do it in silence. Then Bridget Woollard and Mary climbed the hill behind the retreat centre and threw the earth to four winds. Mary comments that, for the women, it was important to have a ritual to mark a leaving behind before they could embark on this historic new beginning. For Mary, the ritual marked a public stance of solidarity with them and defiance with regard to her own, Roman Catholic, Church.

More controversially, symbols are used that connect with pre-Christian spirituality in Britain, insofar as it can be rediscovered, and symbols drawn from the participants' own lives and from nature. For example, during the liturgy to celebrate menarche, the mother offers a gift, saying, 'I give you this sign of the Moon, a waxing Moon to denote your growth towards fullness' (Ward and Wild 1995b: 64).

The fiftieth birthday celebration took place in a circle around a candle, a birthday card and a bowl of roses and plantain. Ruth Burgess comments on the choice of flowers: 'Flowers fragrant and fragile chosen to celebrate love, days of wine and roses and the fullness of life. Plantain, the waybread (Mother of worts, open from Eastward, powerful within. Over you chariots rolled, queens rode, brides cried, bulls belled. All these you withstood[1])—a herb of power and endurance—a type of the spirituality needed for the "long haul"of life' (Burgess 1999).

In all my years of growing up and ministry in congregational churches, 'doing the flowers' has been regarded as the work of the women or ladies. But I can imagine the incomprehension or disgust with which any attempt to give ritual significance to the flowers, particularly female ritual significance, would have been met!

The St Hilda Community pondered on this stock reaction: 'To speak too much of nature and natural processes, like birth and creation, has been deemed by patriarchy as pagan…St Hilda's liturgies consciously work at redeeming these traditions for the church. We draw on sources from the Hebrew Bible, the psalms, and the medieval Christian mystics, as well as from goddess and Celtic material' (Fageol 1991: 24).

Dancing has also been condemned as a ritual act, because it involves bodily contact, and because it removes worship from the control of words. The circle formation arouses deep suspicion, as it devolves the power of leadership and entrusts responsibility to every participant. People who are used to hierarchical seating patterns feel threatened by the notion of shared responsibility. If they are customarily leaders, they do not wish to give power away, and if they are customarily congregational members, they do not wish to take it up. Circles remove the barrier between leader and led, behind which both sets of people feel safe.

Lillalou Hughes , a teacher and exponent of circle dancing, writes that

1.   The Saxon Lay of nine herbs.

circle dancing 'was introduced to Britain at Findhorn in the early seventies by Bernhard Wosein, a German ballet dancer. The dances are drawn from the great wealth of ancient dances of Greece, the Slavic countries, the Jewish and Celtic traditions. These have inspired new compositions and choreography and there are now many new circle dances, sometimes using folk songs and tunes' (Hughes 1991: 32).

In the European and Hebrew traditions Lillalou mentions, the dances were community gatherings, often mimicking domestic rituals, such as collecting water, or providing opportunities for young men and women to meet in a controlled environment. They differ from long or square dances, in that, generally, everyone is participating all the time. A long-ways set dance will have a 'top couple' and often they will be the only ones dancing, or they may dance with the 'second couple'. Similarly, in a square dance, sequences will often be danced by two couples at a time, defined by the 'top couple'. Although the sequence of the dance in the longways set usually means that each couple dances at the top in turn, and although the non-dancing members of the set may well be clapping to the rhythm and whooping, the feeling of the dance for long periods is of standing, watching others dance, waiting your turn, waiting, with a little nervous anticipation, for the point at which all the other dancers will be watching you.

The circle dance and the circle shape are also prophetic. They embody the equality which feminist liturgy proclaims as the model of life. Eco-feminism as a philosophy has challenged anthropocentrism, which places humanity at the pinnacle in a hierarchy of creation. It has entered feminist theology through the creation-centred spirituality championed by Matthew Fox. In rejecting patriarchal theology, feminist theology rejects the whole value system which derives from dualism between spiritual and natural or mental and material realms, giving overriding value to the first, and subjecting and despising the second.

Women have traditionally been associated with the natural, the earthly or the material realm, and consquently have been considered unfit to exercise functions in the higher realm of spirit or mind. In the religious world this has deprived them of authority or priestly function. They have been forbidden, in various ways, to have any contact with what is holy. In the secular world, women have been systematically denied the education or opportunities to engage in intellectual or man-agerial functions.

Feminist thought rejects the duality upon which this discrimination is based. Women have recognized that they are closely connected to the rhythms and cycles of nature. Like the earth, we go through cycles of fertility. We nurture and bring forth new life. Therefore, we do not withdraw from the despised natural realm in order to cultivate our minds. Rather, we honour and rejoice in the wholeness of the world in which we live.

We are not 'masters' of creation, but partners with the cosmos and with God. On the other hand, humans have, and exercise, tremendous destructive power. In the circle, we acknowledge our equal responsibility and power, and we celebrate and acknowledge our oneness with all that is. Much new writing is rich with imagery drawn from the natural world, and offers opportunities to express our shared need for forgiveness for the scars and extinctions it has suffered at our hand.

Human Rites contains a section on 'The Christian Vision', which includes observances for the winter solstice and the new year, and litanies for creation in travail and for the four elements. In each of these, figures and images drawn from nature are mingled with Christian imagery. For example, the link between the northern winter solstice and Christmas, already a mingling of Christian and pagan spirituality, is openly acknowledged with a 'toast' to the sun, followed by a prayer of rejoicing in the light of the world.

Goddess Worship

So far, I have commented on liturgical praxis and theory within a generally Christian setting. I have described some of the enormously varied and rich experience of worshipping communities within this setting. Some of the liturgies draw on imagery and symbolism that are marginal to the Christian setting, and that certainly provoke fearful and hostile reactions among traditional Christians.

Another rich and varied field is that of worshipping or ritual communities that find their spiritual life and ritual symbolism outside the Christian context. Christian feminists attempt to reach back through the thick patriarchal layers of Scripture and tradition to celebrate the living God in the authentic voice of the oppressed as it is heard in Scripture and tradition. While there is certainly a good deal to be discovered in this process, there are many for whom the process is meaningless and doomed to failure, who argue that a thoroughgoing feminist hermeneutic finds the Christian traditions irretrievably patriarchal.

The same principles apply to pagan ritual as to Christian liturgy. It is dead unless it arises from and nourishes an integral community, and powerless if it does not issue in practical passion for justice and the integrity of creation. The difference is that there is not the same weight of dead liturgical practice. As a dominant religion over so much of the world, and throughout so much of history, Christianity has persisted through permitting dead liturgy to sit alongside the fragmentation of community and the perversion of justice. This is by far the norm in Christian practice, and accounts for the deep unpopularity of the Christian churches in some sophisticated northern cultures.

In some cultures where Christianity is growing fastest, particularly in some African countries, it still exists alongside corruption and genocide. Hugh McCullum's book, *The Angels Have Left Us* (1996), chronicles the horrifying events in Rwanda in the 1990s. He notes that more than 90% of the Rwandese population are baptized Christians. The churches were deeply implicated in the massacres, both in their message to local congregations and in the national leadership. Though there were acts of heroism and courageous prophetic voices, in general, the Christian voice was divided or silent. 'Church leaders, who received patronage and lavish gifts from the ruling party, too often remained silent in the face of injustice' (McCullum 1996: 65); 'Church pulpits could have provided an opportunity for almost the entire population to hear a strong message that could have prevented the genocide. Instead, the leaders remained silent' (McCullum 1996: 68).

No doubt, in their time, the rituals of every culture have been used to oppress a populace, to bolster the power of tyrants and to justify cruelty. But the traditions have been so repressed by the domination of Christianity (or other major faiths) that they spring back to life with the vigour of renewal, and the justification of long-silenced voices. Melissa Raphael calls it 'a linguistic, imaginal, textual play with androcentric anthropology, archaeology, mythography and the history of religions in the unpredictable situation of Western women celebrating and sometimes worshipping goddesses for the first time in about 1500 years' (Raphael 1996: 37).

The sense of 'play' resonates through the literature. The celebratory rituals that are described are hugely enjoyable, and touch on the deepest emotions, emotions and enjoyment which are entirely alien to the vast majority of Christian experience. Here, the experience of this kind of ritual tells us, is where women and women's experience is truly at home. Daly defines the profane (originally the area outside a temple, which was not sacred, and therefore 'safe') as the flat foreground of alienation. The sacred is the Background, 'the Realm of Wild Reality; the Homeland of women's Selves and of all Others; the Time/Space where auras of plants, planets, stars, animals, and all Other animate beings connect' (Daly 1993: 1).

There are three elements to this kind of ritual life, which arise from feminist ways of thinking. First, the sacred is female: these are goddess cults and the appropriate term for their discussion is thealogy. Secondly, women's experience, both present and from as much as can be learned from female heritage, forms the structure for ritual practice, which honours the body and its connectedness with the fecund earth. Thirdly, and arising from the second, ritual life resonates with concerns for the environment, not, as in patriarchal science and religion, as the object of man's discovery and manipulation (however benign), but as a connected whole with the practitioners of ritual.

There is no single orthodoxy to pagan spirituality. Indeed, many of the ancient goddess traditions are lost in history. It is hard to find out what form the ritual took, though some artefacts remain, such as statues, and some memories are embedded in the dominant culture, for example, the ancient quarter days and other pagan festivals. Clearly, ancient ritual must, in any case, interact with the present experience of women. There are tensions between the present reality and historical fact, with some groups trying consciously to practise ancient rituals, and others seeking to allow practice to flow far more from the experience of the participants.

Charlene Spretnak describes the early days of discovery of goddess spirituality as an undefined wonder at the riches of what they were finding:

> We discovered powerful female bodies of all sizes honoured and revered; statues that were half bird and half female, linking humanity with the rest of nature, ritual figurines of female bodies incised with representations of life-giving water; symbols of the sacred pelvic triangle of the female; and sacred myths of the transformative powers of the Earth and the female celebrated in ecstatic dance and holy rite. Imagine our surprise (1991: 129).

She goes on to describe the development of interaction between discovery of the traditions with present-day experience: 'The contemporary renaissance of Goddess spirituality draws on a growing body of knowledge about historical Goddess religion but is shaped and energized by the living practice which is both personal and communal, ancient and spontaneous' (Spretnak 1991: 133). Rituals vary in how much and how specifically they draw on the ancient traditions. Celu Amberston sees a progression towards structure:

> In my experience, 'do as you feel' ritual seems to be a stage that most groups go through as they develop, rather than being an end in itself. What I have observed is that most New Age groups (especially women's groups) begin with a 'do as you feel' format, which is intended to break down old patterns of patriarchal authority, but if they stay together long enough, they eventually adopt a more structured format (1995: 30).

Interestingly, she links the development of structures with changes in patterns of authority. 'Women, in particular, resist becoming leaders (of ritual or anything else). This is partly from a lack of self-confidence and partly from a reluctance to recreate anything resembling a patriarchal authority structure. However, those groups that don't choose some kind of structure usually stagnate and die from lack of committed direction and leadership' (Amberston 1995: 30). This relates to the experience of the St Hilda Community, cited earlier in the chapter, working in a Christian context.

Much of the ritual is informal and sometimes domestic, celebrating the passages of women's lives from girlhood to mature womanhood to 'croning', the celebration of post-menopausal age in a rediscovery of older traditions of women's design and leadership of rituals in the home.

Charlene Spretnak describes a menarche ritual for her daughter, which follows a traditional structure but allows the content to develop from the experience of the participants. There are seven movements, enumerated by Celu Amberston (Amberston 1995: 54-55): planning the ceremony; preparation of the ceremony; creating the sacred space; the cleansing and blessing; the opening of the ritual; the body of the ritual; the conclusion of the ritual.

These steps are not exactly mirrored in Spretnak's description, but there is a definite sense of prescribed movement through a logical pattern. The ritual includes: gathering the people and arranging the space with symbols and favourite objects; a preparation of the girls and women with singing, fragrance, touching, painting foreheads; the body of the ritual lies in telling stories, laughing and crying; after this, the women form a 'birth canal', through which the girls pass, being hugged and kissed on the way, to emerge as women; the ritual ends with giving of gifts and feasting.

Kathleen McPhillips describes a girlhood to womanhood ritual for the daughters of some women in her community, reflecting on the ritual specifically in the light of Raphael's arguments. She compares the ritual planned within her community of friends with the way she learned about womanhood. Her mother taught her about menstruation as a clinical fact, but, 'the only time it was explained within a religious context was during the mother and daughter night at school when Sr Margaret suggested a very dubious link between menstruation and the Hail Mary which left me baffled for years afterwards' (McPhillips 1998: 17).

She describes the event surrounding the ritual, which is to take place at a camp with three women and their daughters in the Australian outback. The women experience all kinds of problems as they separate themselves temporarily from the routines of their family lives. Once together, the strength of womanhood is affirmed as the three families work together to set up a camp and get a meal together. The ritual itself draws on a variety of symbols and stories. After all, there is no set of texts and traditions for such an event, a fact that McPhillips finds both grieving and liberating.

The ritual takes place in the wilderness, in a liminal space between community and privacy. As she reflects, McPhillips sees this as valuable in creating a bond between the women and the girls. But she also laments the lack of a public celebration. She writes, 'it seems that the importance of the public sphere is that rituals take place before others as a sign of social solidarity and acceptance' (1998: 26). The fact that there is no tradition of 'conscious organized rituals for moving through life's passages' (McPhillips 1998: 26) which affirms women's and men's bodily sacredness means that private ceremony is always in conflict with public and social pressures.

This tension can be seen in a prenuptial ritual, described by Spretnak, which is powerful with sensual and erotic movement. The bride is led along a path of rose petals to a bath of scented water, where she is left alone, while the other women wait. When she is ready, the bride rejoins the women, who 'encircle her, massaging oil into her warm, soft body while we take turns reading favorite poems of eros softly near her ear' (Spretnak 1991: 148). She records her own experience:

> I was given that ritual before my remarriage. The following day, still enveloped with the glow of grace and transformation, I thought back to the bridal showers I had attended during my college years and just after: ladies in cheery frocks playing parlor games, partaking of tea and cake,

> chatting of just about anything on the eve of marriage except the elemen-
> tal bounteousness of the female, skimming on the surface of our lives
> (Spretnak 1991: 149).

The bridal shower perfectly exemplifies Daly's definition of the profane. It serves to alienate the bride from the depth and power of her
own experience, hiding the wonder of the situation by remaining on the
bright, shiny surface. The prenuptial ritual delves into the sacred, finding
the woman among women at home in her own spirituality, and the
mystery at the depth of experience.

Rituals such as these are prophetic in all kinds of ways. Where
women and men see rituals developing around the rites of passage of
women's lives, they may become aware of the need for similar rituals for
men. Brian Wren writes of the need to develop a non-patriarchal concept of maleness, male identity and male spirituality. Ruether says that,
'There remain important areas where specifically male rites of passage
need to be written, such as puberty rites for young males and retirement
for older males. These…must be written by men. The formation of a
new perspective on these critical points of male development awaits the
rising of communities of males who are engaged in their own exodus
from patriarchy in solidarity with feminist women' (Ruether 1985: 182).

This is truly prophetic, since rituals that encompass male and female
experience in non-patriarchal celebration point the way to an entirely
new way of being human. The potential for a new human community
may be eschatological, in the sense of being an actually unrealizable
ideal. Perhaps it is not even an ideal, and men are incapable of being
released from patriarchy. But, if it will stand scrutiny as an ideal, like
Whitehead's divine 'lure' (see p. 111), the ideal can inform what we do
and draw us towards its fulfilment.

Another way in which rituals of this kind are prophetic is in challenging the prejudices and taboos of ordinary life. Menses, pregnancy and
lactation, hidden and feared generally, are now celebrated. Ways of living that do not conform to rigid patriarchal patterns are acknowledged
and celebrated. Rosemary Radford Ruether describes rites of healing,
for example, after rape (which also includes a ritual bath, but with a
different significance), after abortion and a coming out rite for a lesbian.
She reflects:

> Official Christian ethics rejects both premarital and extramarital sexuality,
> attempting to make the first sexual intercourse ('deflowering') of the
> female coincide with her wedding night. Throughout much of Christian

history, the church forbade contraception for married couples. The woman was expected to be sexually available to her husband on demand; she was not allowed to define her own sexual needs. Marriage was expected to be permanent, and divorce was rejected by most Christians until recently. All these values are in disrepute at the present time, yet there continue to be both a great need and a longing for committed and faithful relationships that can build new families and provide stability for people throughout their lives (1985: 192).

As more and more deeply significant moments in life find ritual expression, the fabric of prejudice is gradually unpicked. At my own church, the discussion of a request for a same-sex commitment ceremony brought people face to face with their professed liberality. Without a rise in the practice of ceremonies for different lifestyles, the couple in question would not have approached us. Our experience was part of the prophetic action of new ritual practice.

Again, the rituals may awaken awareness of a complex of injustices. Because oppression is complex, women who engage in rituals which arise from their own experience as oppressed people may find that their consciousness of being oppressors is raised. McPhillips recognizes the incongruity of her own liberating experience, taking place on 'land, once the land of the ingenous Awabakal people', while, 'The symbols we will use in the ritual derive from western myths and stories which took place thousands of miles from where we are and we are all white' (1998: 20). She recognizes the injustice of this: 'Race is the silent context here…our context is…profoundly shaped by past and current violence against the Awabakal people' (1998: 20).

But, above all, these rituals affirm and strengthen women in their own identity and power. They are part of the long, slow, painful struggle back to personhood from the abuse done to us by a society that silences our voices, takes away our chance for the fulfilment of our potential and subjects us to psychological and, sometimes, physical violence. These rituals allow us to recover our bodies from the shame that society heaps upon our natural functions. Women may arise with their own dignity and power from these rituals, and challenge the world.

Like the excitement of rediscovery in the Christian community, the literature describing Goddess spirituality is filled with exultation. Zsusanna Budapest speaks of 'A new kind of trust', which she sees as, 'the most important contribution that women's spirituality has to give to the women's movement. We learned we can trust our bodies when we learned we had the right to control them. We are learning we can trust our souls through learning that our right to have them is rooted in our recognition of the Goddess, of the female principle within the universe and ourselves' (1986: 4).

Raphael sees this a a renewal of life: 'Female sacral acts regenerate or re-energize what has lost its life or energy by desecration and profanization. For if profanization of the sacred is destructive of its object, then its opposite, sacralization, returns the natural potency or inner *telos* to the object in an act closely akin to re-creation' (1996: 43).

So far, the sense of play, of delight, of discovery and of freedom has leapt out from these rituals. They are full of enjoyment and it is up to the participants to weave their own tapestry from their experiences and their choice from the traditions. There are many traditions from which to draw ritual and imagery: pre-Christian European witchcraft; African-based folk religions of the Caribbean or Brazil; the pagan religions still extant in Africa; folk religions of other indigenous peoples, such as the native Americans; old classical religions such as those of ancient Greece. The pick 'n' mix culture of the postmodern West encourages women to draw from different traditions, to wear a dream-catcher and celebrate beltane, to spend an evening dancing circle dances from Israel, Europe, Polynesia and Africa.

Of course, this has always happened, as cultures mixed and, in particular, when elements of an older religion have been incorporated into a new dominant religion. Christianity has embedded in it elements of pre-Christian pagan worship in Europe, which have been transported around the world on the wings of mission and empire and themselves been used to repress other old religions. For example, Australian Christians celebrate the winter solstice by eating food appropriate to it, and singing carols about the light coming into the world, at the height of summer, having repressed whatever seasonally appropriate celebrations the indigenous peoples had as part of their tradition.

The Virgin Mary has famously taken on the characteristics of many local goddess figures. Early depictions owed much to mother goddesses of classical pantheons. More recently, in Guadalupe, the indigenous cult of the Goddess Coatlalopeuh was suppressed by the Aztecs. Coatl means a serpent and this was a serpent Goddess. In 1531, a poor Indian man had a vision of Maria Coatlalopeuh, at the place where another Goddess, Tonantsi, had been worshipped. The Catholic Church named her as mother of God and she was taken into the existing cult of Mary.

Elsewhere, the institutional Church has taken over sites and stories which derive from pre-Christian paganism. All over the Celtic fringes of Britain there are sacred sites and hagiographical stories which relate to pre-Christian roots. A case in point is St Winefride's Well, Holywell, in Wales. I visited this site with a group of women from the Free Church Women's Council, and its history is a fascinating interweaving of female sacredness and male imposition.

The well stands under a heavy ancient stone housing; the water is incredibly clear. Worn stone images peer from the arches. On the day we visited, there was a voluptuous Latin American woman, waist deep in the water, her leggings showing off her stunning figure to great effect. Behind her was a Welsh TV crew. Her story was that she had been crippled with arthritis until she was cured by a visit to St Winefride's Well some years previously. Now she revisits every year. The film crew interviewed her as she was, waist deep in the water, for a documentary on S4C. The Free Church ladies were delighted. Before going to buy St Winefride pens and candles, one or two took their shoes off and dipped their feet in the water to see whether they could obtain healing for arthritis and other ills. They gasped at the coldness of the water, and the daring of Free Church women bathing at a Catholic shrine.

The Christian origins of the well go back to 660 CE, to the story of a young woman who defended her virginity against a lustful nobleman, Caradoc. Eventually, he lashed out in anger and cut her head off with his sword. From the spot where the head fell, a spring of water started to flow. Her uncle, Beuno, who witnessed the violence, picked up her head and set it on the shoulders of her corpse. She was immediately restored to life, with only a thin scar round her neck to show where the nobleman's sword had cut. Winefride became a nun and was eventually abbess of a convent at Gwytherin near Llanrwst.

The well was later enclosed by the present heavy stone shrine. It is no more than seven feet high, and only just wide enough for two people to pass. The water is fed into a broad shallow pool, where the Free Church women were bathing their feet, but there is an ancient gateway, allowing one person at a time (possibly with a helper) to descend into the narrow space where the suppliant might enter for healing. The overall impression is of the bright sparkling water trapped under a squat weight of stones, controlling access to the blessing, and making the once bright hillside gloomy and ominous.

About a century ago, the waters of St Winefride's Well stopped flowing for the first time in 2000 years. A mineshaft had diverted the underground stream which fed the spring, and the waters dried up. The well, the magic, the tourists—the power threatened to cease it all for ever. However, the mining company rebuilt the channel, and the mysterious water was saved from the disruptive power of industry.

Of course, many of the Celtic saints derive from older deities, marking the numinous qualities of woods, mountains and, above all, life-giving springs. There are no records of the pre-Christian Winefride or of the earlier mythology on which the very Christian story of defended chastity may have been based. But there is enormous attraction in the ancient Celtic veneration of nature, threads of which may survive in what is still accessible in the roots of Celtic Christianity. The tradition of passing through the water of the well three times for healing may be associated with the Celtic tradition of baptism by triple immersion, which, in turn, may have deeper and older roots.

The overall effect of the visit to St Winefride's Well was a mixture of superstition, fun, nostalgia, media circus and serious spiritual experience. But the danger of pick 'n' mix is that nothing genuinely new happens. The very term, 'post', used as in 'post-Christian' and 'postmodern', suggests a relationship with the tradition from which the person is passing on. Celu Amberston comments that, 'When ungrounded people change their religion, usually it is only their beliefs that change, and not the ways in which they practice them. Unconsciously they must fall back upon the old ritual form with which they are most familiar—in most cases, the Judeo-Christian one' (1995: 5). She warns that modern pagans are not taking their spirituality seriously and criticizes that sense of playing a game.

This is because there are dangers as well as positive aspects to the forces released in ritual, particularly where magic is involved. She writes:

> they are unaware of the potential dangers involved in tampering, even superficially, with the magic arts. Some of the danger that modern Pagans may be unaware of (or disregard) include the boomerang effect, the possibility of psychic attack, the effects of leaving oneself ungrounded after a ritual, and the unwanted effects that may occur if the intent of the ceremony is either harmful or unclear (Amberston 1995: 15).

To counter these dangers, Amberston provides a collection of resources and practical advice. She describes a pattern for sacred dance, with a long process of preparation for the sacred space and the participants, and with the opportunity to move between the intensity of the

central dance and quieter, more reflective spaces. She suggests celebrating the cross-quarter days—Samhain, Imholg, Beltane and Lughnasadh—
as she feels that they are, 'more Earth-centred, female-centred holidays,
rather than the solar Male-centred rituals of the Sun-cycle' (1995: 64).
And she describes rituals, continuing over several days, for these periods.

Her intention is to enable present-day pagans to use all the wealth of
the old traditions, but with their own spiritual development in mind.
She describes what might happen to an ancient prayer: 'Oh, great mystery, give me strength, that my people may live'. She says that a modern
secular prayer might be, 'Oh, God, give me strength so that I may live
and acquire more material goods'. A modern New Age prayer would
be, 'Oh, God or Goddess, give me strength to discover more about
myself and grow spiritually'. The people have disappeared and the new
spirituality focuses on the individual.

This is very much the emphasis of Amberston's rituals. While she is
keen to recapture the ritual as a group-forming experience, in fact, the
rituals, their purpose and the preparation for them are described very
much from the point of view of the individual. This is not true of all
goddess worship that appears in the literature. Some rituals reach out
beyond the participating community with the intention of challenging
or healing a wider community.

A ritual at Greenham Common was effective in strengthening and
grounding the women who participated in it, but also confronted those
who watched it with the power of the women and their well-grounded
concern for the world in which such destructive forces were deployed as
a matter of course. In some rituals there is a strong sense of oneness with
the world. June Boyce-Tillman has devised a participative musical
performance called 'The Healing of the Earth', which will involve the
audience as performer, out of which she believes real healing energy will
come.

In any case, witchcraft and goddess worship has been subversive
throughout its long repression by patriarchal religions. It was at one time
possible for the old religions to survive alongside Christianity. But they
were brutally suppressed during the witchcraze that swept Europe
through the thirteenth and fourteenth centuries, part of the overall
silencing of women which also shut Christian women mystics and
prophets in closed communities. Starhawk laments, 'Memory of the true
craft faded everywhere except within the hidden covens. With it, went
the memory of women's heritage and history, of our ancient roles as

leaders, teachers, healers, seers. Lost, also, was the conception of the Great Spirit, as manifest in nature, in life, in woman. Mother Goddess slept, leaving the world to the less than gentle rule of the God-Father' (1992: 262).

Now, the silence is being broken. The ancient powers are stirring. Women are finding their strength and dignity again. Starhawk goes on, 'The Goddess has at last stirred from sleep, and women are re-awakening to our ancient power. The feminist movement, which began as a political, economic, and social struggle, is opening to a spiritual dimension. In the process, many women are discovering the old religion, reclaiming the word *witch* and, with it, some of our lost culture' (1992: 262).

With the rise of goddess worship, there is an image and sacred role for women which is ours alone. This gives rise to women who are strong in their own identity, sure of their place in a heritage of women's power, and confident enough to exercise a subversive role openly and without fear and shame. They appear in the literature as the Warrior Woman and the Wild Woman. One of the images used for the re-awakening male identity is the Wild Man, who is in tune with the great forests. The Wild Man is caged by patriarchal suppression of true masculinity, and must be released by recognizing and overcoming patriarchy, a task which is arguably more difficult for men, who benefit so hugely from it.

The Wild Woman is also caged. But she emerges as an assertive confident creature. In *Women who Run with the Wolves* (1992), Clarissa Pinkola Estés describes her. 'She must shake out her pelt, strut the old pathways, assert her instinctual knowledge. We can all assert our membership of the ancient scar clan, proudly bear the battle scars of our time, write our secrets on walls, refuse to be ashamed, lead the way through and out' (Estés 1992: 460). The prophetic element of spirituality shows itself in the leadership of those who have found the way. She ends with a clarion call: 'Let us not overspend on anger. Instead let us be empowered by it. Most of all let us be cunning with our feminine wits' (Estés 1992: 460).

The powerful woman has the strength to be truly prophetic, that is, to open up genuinely new ways. Christina Feldman writes, 'The warrior spirit is not concerned with reversing positions of dominance or acting out new hierarchies but with transformation of values, assumptions and structures that perpetuate dominance, subjugation and exploitation' (1994: 221). For her, the Warrior Woman is the Feminist Mystic, who is confident of her physical and spiritual identity and power and, there-fore, an agency of change.

It will be interesting to see how much interaction there will be in coming years between the massive energy which is being released in these different spheres of ritual and liturgy. Will Christian churches, as in other instances, allow pagan sources to influence them, bringing wisdom and energy from women's spirituality? Will the explosion of new imagery and rediscovered tradition within the Christian world transform patterns of worship and expectations of inclusivity? What kinds of osmosis will take place at the porous margins, or thresholds between cultures?

Conclusion

These are exciting times to be living in!

There is an enormous wealth of creativity flowing from a great variety of different cultures and background. Christian feminist, womanist, *mujerista*, dalit, creationist—all interact through material for worship and practice of spirituality. Around the fringes of Christian experience is a whole boundary for interaction with Gaia spirituality and goddess worship, which form their own centres for exploration.

Symbols and actions flow back and forth across the boundaries, enabling either a pick 'n' mix compilation of material or studies of cultural connection. In a postmodern age, neither pattern can be valued over the other.

The continuum stretches all the way from the traditional church or women's meeting learning to be open to new metaphors in a traditional setting, to covens gathering to re-enact ancient rites in a modern context. Even the continuum is not a single journey. The connections and lines are fluid.

Part of the challenge lies not in the invention of new ways, but in the discovery of what has alway been there, and been hidden or perverted. The stories of women from Scripture speak in the ways they were always intended to speak. The fact of their generations-long silence is an injustice which has impoverished women and men. God bustles out of Scripture with the energy of the charlady, the ferocity of the mother bear and the practicality of the midwife. Wisdom is her daughter and playful bosom-friend. The fact of God's effemination (loss of femininity, formed on the pattern of emasculation) is the excuse for male domination and the near destruction of the planet.

Through the centuries, and despite the crushing pressure of suppression, women have spoken, written and acted in powerful and creative ways. The current generation is rediscovering women's traditions as a matter of celebration as well as finding out how severe has been their repression. A deep, abiding anger, which recognizes that we have the right not to forgive some of the worst human sins, comes out of the same energy which rejoices in the strength of women.

We gather our stories in compilations of liturgies and sermons, in ongoing publications and the litter of worship material which floats from ritual to ritual around the networks which form from time to time. Women gather themselves in great conferences and local groups, to experiment and find their own meaning.

Scholars chart progress, reminding us of our heritage. Liturgists capture brilliant ideas and turn them into reality. Artists and architects express new ways of worshipping in new forms of space. Prophets clash with old ecclesial authorities and scandalize received morality. And out of it all comes the recognition of an alternative way of being. Tradition told us to submit, to be silent and passive, and by accepting the traditional role, we allowed injustice and violence free reign. When women and the oppressed of the world are no longer silent but speak and sing and dance, injustice must find its limit, and the community of promise come close.

Above all, to be part of all this is the inestimable privilege of life. When I dance with the circle dancers, or get swept up in a group-hug after a howled lament; when I write or read new words, full of beauty and light; when I participate in putting together an act of worship that reaches into people's hearts and weaves their emotions into a web of awe; even when the cold water of someone else's justifiable anger is dashed into my face, I cannot believe how good it is to be woman among women, and I cannot grasp the enormity of what has been lost to the world when women have been crushed.

Bibliography

Aikin, A. (later Anna Laetitia Barbauld)
    1781   *Hymns in Prose for Children*: (London: J. Johnson).
Aikin, L. (ed.)
    1825   *The Works of Anna Laetitia Barbauld with a Memoir by Lucy Aikin* (2 vols.; London: Longman & Co).
Amberston, C.
    1995   *Deepening the Power: Community, Ritual and Sacred Theatre* (Victoria, BC: Beach Holme Publications).
Amoah, E.
    1995   'Theology from the Perspective of African Women', in Ortega 1995: 1-7.
Bailey, J. (ed.)
    1971   *New Life: Songs and Hymns for Assemblies, Clubs and Churches* (Great Yarmouth: Galliard).
Barbauld, A.L.
    1781   *Hymns in Prose for Children* (3rd edn).
    1792   'Remarks on Mr Gilbert Wakefield's Enquiry into the Expediency and Propriety of Public or Social Worship', in Aikin 1825: I,413-70.
    1793   'Sins of Government, Sins of the Nation, or A Discourse for the Fast appointed on April 19 1773', in Aikin 1825: II, 379-412.
Barclay, W.
    1956   *The Gospel of Matthew*, I (The Daily Study Bible; Edinburgh: The Saint Andrew Press).
Bible Society, British and Foreign
    1998   *Faith Comes by Hearing* (Swindon, 1998).
Black, M.
    1973   *Romans* (New Century Bible; London: Oliphants).
Boisclair, R.A.
    1994   'Amnesia in the Catholic Sunday Lectionary: Women—Silenced from the Memories of Salvation History', in Hinsdale and Kaminski 1994: 109-137.
Boulding, E.
    1992   *The Underside of History: A View of Women through Time* (Sage, 2nd edn).
Bowie, F.
    1995   'Beguines' in Isherwood and McEwan 1995: 16-17.
Boyce Tillman J., and J. Wootton (eds.)
    1993   *Reflecting Praise* (London: Stainer & Bell).
Boyce Tillman, J.
    1998   'Interview' *Feminist Theology* 18: 97-117.

Brock, S.
    1990   'The Holy Spirit as Feminine in Early Syriac Literature', in Soskice 1990:
                73-89.
Brooke, E.
    1993   *A Woman's Book of Shadows: Witchcraft, a Celebration* (London: Women's
                Press).
Budapest, Z.
    1986   *The Holy Book of Women's Mysteries* (Oakland, CA).
Burgess, R.
    1999   'Celebrating a 50th Birthday', *Worship Live* 15: 10.
Byatt, A.
    1992   *Angels and Insects* (London: Chatho & Windus).
Bynum, C.
    1987   *Holy Feast, Holy Fast: The Religious Significance of Food to Medieval Women*
                (Berkeley: University of California Press).
Byrne, L. (ed.)
    1991   *The Hidden Tradition* (London: SPCK).
    1992   *Christian Women Together* (London: CCBI).
'Carol'
    1994   'My Story, my Song' in Walton and Durber 1994: 54-58.
Carr, D.
    1990   *Towards an Asian Theology of Hope: Bible Studies Prepared by Dyanchand Carr*
                (Hong Kong: The Christian Conference of Asia).
Christ, C., and J. Plaskow (eds.)
    1992   *Womanspirit Rising: A Feminist Reader in Religion* (San Francisco: Harper-
                SanFrancisco, 2nd edn).
Christ, C.
    1992a   'Spiritual Quest and Women's Experience', in Christ and Plaskow 1992:
                226-48.
    1992b   'Why Women Need the Goddess', in Christ and Plaskow (eds.) 1992:
                273-86.
Cooey, P.
    1994   *Religious Imagination and the Body: A Feminist Analysis* (Oxford: Oxford
                University Press).
Copeland, M.
    1994   'Toward a Christian Feminist Theology of Solidarity', in Hinsdale and
                Kaminski 1994: 3-38.
Cotes, M.
    1994   'Standing in the Stable', in Walton and Durber (eds.) 1994: 6-8.
Crawford, J., and M. Kinnamon (eds.)
    1983   *In God's Image: Reflections on Identity, Human Wholeness and the Authority of*
                Scripture (Geneva: WCC Publications).
Cross, F.L., and E.A. Livingstone (eds.)
    1974   *The Oxford Dictionary of the Christian Church* (Oxford: Oxford University
                Press).
Daly, M.
    1993   *Outercourse: The Bedazzling Voyage, Containing Recollections from my Logbook*
                of a Radical Feminist Philosopher (London: Women's Press).

Downing, C.
      1992   *Women's Mysteries* (New York: Crossroad).
      1996   *The Goddess: Mythological Images of the Feminine* (New York: Continuum).
Estés, Clarissa Pinkola
      1992   *Women Who Run with Wolves: Contacting the Wild Woman* (London:
                  Rider).
Fageol, S.
      1991   'Celebrating Experience', in St Hilda Community 1991: 16-26.
Feldman, C.
      1994   *The Quest of the Warrior Woman: Women as Mystics, Healers and Guides*
                  (London: Aquarium).
Furlong, M.
      1991   'Introduction: A "Non-Sexist" Community', in St Hilda Community
                  1991: 5-15.
Gray, G.
      1977   *Joshua, Judges and Ruth* (New Century Bible; London: Marshall, Morgan &
                  Scott).
Hayes, D.L.
      1995   *Hagar's Daughers: Womanist Ways of Being in the World* (New York: Paulist
                  Press)
Hilten, W. van, M. Koijck-de Bruijne, E. Silcocks (eds.),
      1984   *Eva's Lied* (Kampen: Kok).
Hinsdale, M., and P. Kaminski (eds.)
      1994   *Women and Theology* (Maryknoll, NY: Orbis Books).
Hughes, L.
      1991   'Finding our Balance: Dance at St Hilda's', in St Hilda Community 1991:
                  32-33.
Isasi-Díaz, A.
      1995   'Elements of a *Mujerista* Anthropology', in O'Hara Graff 1995: 90-104.
Isherwood, L., and D. McEwan, (eds.)
      1995   *An A to Z of Feminist Theology* (Sheffield: Sheffield Academic Press).
Jackson,P.
      1994   'Celebration', *Worship Live* introductory issue (autum): 21-22.
Kennedy, M.
      1994   'Invisible Christians', in Walton and Durber 1994: 13-20.
      1995   'Christian Survivors of Sexual Abuse (CSSA) Retreat October 1994'
                  Worship Live 1.1 (spring 1995): 3.
Kerr, P.
      1997   'What Are You Hearing at the Back?' (Fellowship Paper 102 College of
                  Preachers, Bourne, Lincolnshire): 7-13.
Knödel, N.
      1997   'Reconsidering an Obsolete Rite', *Feminist Theology* 14: 106-125.
Laffey, A.
      1990   *Wives, Harlots and Concubines* (London: SPCK).
Lee-Park, S.
      1995   'A Short History of Asian Feminist Theology', in Ortega 1995: 37-48.

Bibliography   139

Liveris, L.B.
    1995   'Feminist Ecclesiology: An Orthodox Perspective from Australia', in
                Ortega 1995: 152-63.
MacHaffie, B.
    1986   *Her Story: Women in Christian Tradition* (Philadelphia: Fortress Press).
Mananzan, M.-J.
    1995   'Feminist Theology in Asia', in Ortega 1995: 29-36.
McCullum, H.
    1996   *The Angels Have Left Us: The Rwandan Tragedy and the Churches* (Risk
                Book Series, 66; Geneva: WCC Publications).
McKenna, M.
    1994   *Not Counting Women and Children: Neglected Stories from the Bible*
                (Tunbridge Wells: Burns & Oates).
McPhillips, K.
    1998   'Rituals, Bodies and Thealogy: Some Questions', *Feminist Theology* 18:
                9-28.
McReynolds, S., and A. O'Hara Graff
    1995   'Sin: When Women are the Context', in O'Hara Graff 1995: 161-72.
Moody, L.A.
    1994   'Toward a Methodology for Doing Theology across the Boundaries of Dif-
                ference: Feminist Theory Meets Feminist Theology', in Hinsdale and
                Kaminski 1994: 186-201.
Morley, J.
    1992   *Bread of Tomorrow: Praying with the World's Poor* (London: SPCK).
Morley, J., and H. Ward (eds.)
    1986   *Celebrating Women* (London: Women in Theology and the Movement for
                the Ordination of Women).
Morton, N.
    1992   'The Dilemma of Celebration', in Christ and Plaskow 1992: 159-66.
Oduyoye, M.
    1990   *Who Will Roll the Stone Away?* (Geneva: WCC Publications).
    1992   *The Will to Arise: Women, Tradition and the Church in Africa* (Maryknoll,
                NY: Orbis Books).
O'Hara Graff, A.
    1994   'Ecclesial Discernment: Women's Voices, New Voices and the Revelatory
                Process', in Hinsdale and Kaminski 1994: 202-215.
O'Hara Graff, A. (ed.)
    1995   *In the Embrace of God: Feminist Approaches to Theological Anthropology*
                (Maryknoll, NY: Orbis Books).
Oliveira, R. de
    1995   'Feminist Theology in Brazil', in Ortega 1995: 65-76.
Ortega, O. (ed.)
    1995   *Women's Visions: Theological Reflection, Celebration, Actions* (Geneva: WCC
                Publications).
Perera, M.
    1995   'An Asian Feminist Ecclesiology', in Ortega 1995: 49-51.

Plaskow, J., and C. Christ (eds.)
    1989   *Weaving the Visions: New Patterns in Feminist Spirituality* (San Francisco: HarperSanFrancisco).
Raphael, M.
    1996   *Thealogy and Embodiment: The Post-Patriarchal Reconstruction of Female Sacrality* (Sheffield: Sheffield Academic Press).
Rattigan, M.
    1995   'Korean Women Theologians: An Observer's Appreciation', in Hinsdale and Kaminski 1995: 156-76.
Rothschild, S.
    1995   'YHWH: A Women's Perspective', in Isherwood and McEwan 1995: 245
Ropeti, M.
    1995   'Feminist Theology: A View from the Pacific', in Ortega 1995: 172-76.
Ruether, R. Radford
    1985   *Women-Church: Theology and Practice of Feminist Liturgical Communities* (London: Harper & Row).
St Hilda Community
    1991   *Women Included: A Book of Services and Prayers* (London: SPCK).
Schlueter, C.J.
    1995   'Feminist Homiletics: Strategies for Empowerment', in Ortega 1995: 138-51.
Schüssler Fiorenza, E.
    1985   *Women Invisible in Society and Church* (Edinburgh: T. & T. Clark).
    1992   'Feminist Spirituality, Christian Identity, and Catholic Vision', in Christ and Plaskow (1992): 136-48.
Soskice, J. Martin (ed.)
    1990   *After Eve* (London: Marshall Pickering).
Spender, D.
    1985   *Man Made Language* (London: Routledge).
Spouge, J.
    1994   'What Do You Want to Be When You Grow Up?', *Worship Live* (introductory issue autumn): 2.
Spretnak, C.
    1982   *The Politics of Women's Spirituality* (New York: Doubleday).
    1991   *States of Grace: The Recovery of Meaning in the Post Modern Age* (San Francisco: HarperSanFrancisco).
Starhawk
    1992   'Witchcraft and Women's Culture', in Christ and Plaskow 1992: 259-68.
Tamez, E.
    1995   'Latin American Feminist Hermeneutics: A Retrospective', in Ortega 1995: 77-89.
Theobald, B.
    1997   'Music in Roman Catholic Liturgies in England and Wales since Vatican II' (PhD Thesis, King Alfred's College).
Trible, P.
    1992a   'Eve and Adam: Genesis 2-3 Reread', in Christ and Plaskow 1992: 74-83.
    1992b   *Texts of Terror* (London: SCM Press).

Tucker, C.
    1994   *Prophetic Sisterhood: Liberal Women Ministers of the Frontier, 1880–1930*
                (Bloomington: Indiana University Press)
Walton, H., and S. Durber (eds.)
    1994   *Silence in Heaven* (London: SCM Press).
Walton, H.
    1994   'Hebrew Women/Egyptian Women', in Walton and Durber 1994: 72-76.
Ward, H., and J. Wild
    1995a   *Guard the Chaos* (London: Darton, Longman & Todd).
    1995b   *Human Rites: Worship Resources for an Age of Change* (London: Mowbray).
Warrior, R.
    1997   'God the Conqueror [8 June]', *Journeying: Prayer Handbook 1997* (London:
                United Reformed Church).
Whitehead, A.
    1979   *Process and Reality* (London: Collier MacMillan, rev. edn).
Willard, F.
    1978   *Woman in the Pulpit* (Washington: Zenger [1889]).
Williams, D.
    1989   'Womanist Theology', in Plaskow and Christ 1989: 179-86.
    1995   'Womanist Theology', in Ortega 1995: 112-26.
Women in Theology (ed.)
    1988   *Who Are You Looking for?* (London: Women in Theology).
Wootton, J. (ed.)
    1999   *Union Chapel: Stability and Change* (London: Union Chapel, 2nd edn).
Wren, B.
    1989   *What Language Shall I Borrow* (London: SCM Press).
    1997   'Glimpses of Holiness', *Worship Live* 2.3 (spring 1997): 5-6.
Yong, R.
    1975   *Analytical Concordance to the Holy Bible* (Guildford and London: United
                Society for Christian Literature, 8th edn).

                                Hymn Books

    1983   *Hymns and Psalms* (prepared by representatives of the British Methodist
                Conference *et al*. London: Methodist Publishing House).
    1992   *Alleluia Aotearoa: Hymns and Songs for all the Churches* (New Zealand
                Hymns Book Trust, Christ Church).
    1998   *Common Ground: A Song Book for All the Churches* (St Andrew Press:
                Edinburgh)

INDEXES

INDEX OF REFERENCES

Old Testament

New Testament

INDEX OF AUTHORS

FEMINIST THEOLOGY TITLES

Individual Titles in Feminist Theology

Linda Hogan, *From Women's Experience to Feminist Theology*

Lisa Isherwood and Dorothea McEwan (eds.), *An A–Z of Feminist Theology*

Lisa Isherwood and Dorothea McEwan, *Introducing Feminist Theology*

Kathleen O'Grady, Ann L. Gilroy and Janette Patricia Gray (eds.), *Bodies, Lives, Voices: Gender in Theology*

Melissa Raphael, *Thealogy and Embodiment: The Post-Patriarchal Reconstruction of Female Sacrality*

Deborah Sawyer and Diane Collier (eds.), *Is There a Future for Feminist Theology?*

Introductions in Feminist Theology

Rosemary Ruether, *Introducing Redemption in Christian Feminism*

Lisa Isherwood and Elizabeth Stuart, *Introducing Body Theology*

Melissa Raphael, *Introducing Thealogy: Discourse on the Goddess*

Pui-lan Kwok, *Introducing Asian Feminist Theology*

Janet H. Wootton, *Introducing a Practical Feminist Theology of Worship*

Feminist Companion to the Bible (1st Series)

Athalya Brenner (ed.), *A Feminist Companion to the Song of Songs*

Athalya Brenner (ed.), *A Feminist Companion to Genesis*

Athalya Brenner (ed.), *A Feminist Companion to Ruth*

Athalya Brenner (ed.), *A Feminist Companion to Judges*

Athalya Brenner (ed.), *A Feminist Companion to Samuel–Kings*

Athalya Brenner (ed.), *A Feminist Companion to Exodus–Deuteronomy*

Athalya Brenner (ed.), *A Feminist Companion to Esther, Judith and Susanna*

Athalya Brenner (ed.), *A Feminist Companion to the Latter Prophets*

Athalya Brenner (ed.), *A Feminist Companion to the Wisdom Literature*

Athalya Brenner (ed.), *A Feminist Companion to the Hebrew Bible in the New Testament*

Athalya Brenner and Carole Fontaine (eds.), *A Feminist Companion to Reading the Bible: Approaches, Methods and Strategies*

Feminist Companion to the Bible (2nd Series)

Athalya Brenner and Carole Fontaine (eds.), *Wisdom and Psalms*

Athalya Brenner (ed.), *Genesis*

Athalya Brenner (ed.), *Judges*

Athalya Brenner (ed.), *Ruth and Esther*

Athalya Brenner (ed.), *Samuel and Kings*